THE DEUTERO-PAULINE LETTERS

Proclamation Commentaries

Matthew, Jack Dean Kingsbury
(Second Edition, Revised and Enlarged)

Mark, Paul J. Achtemeier
(Second Edition, Revised and Enlarged)

Luke, Frederick W. Danker
(Second Edition, Revised and Enlarged)

Jesus Christ in Matthew, Mark, and Luke
Jack Dean Kingsbury

John, D. Moody Smith
(Second Edition, Revised and Enlarged)

Acts
Gerhard Krodel

Paul and His Letters, Leander E. Keck
(Second Edition, Revised and Enlarged)

*The Deutero-Pauline Letters: Ephesians,
Colossians, 2 Thessalonians, 1–2 Timothy, Titus*
J. Paul Sampley, Arland J. Hultgren,
Gerhard Krodel, Walter Taylor
(Revised Edition)

Christology in Paul and John
Robin Scroggs

Revelation: Vision of a Just World
Elisabeth Schüssler Fiorenza

PROCLAMATION COMMENTARIES

Revised Edition

The Deutero-Pauline Letters

Ephesians, Colossians, 2 Thessalonians, 1-2 Timothy, Titus

Gerhard Krodel, Editor

FORTRESS PRESS **MINNEAPOLIS**

THE DEUTERO-PAULINE LETTERS
Ephesians, Colossians, 2 Thessalonians, 1–2 Timothy, Titus
Revised Edition

Library of Congress Cataloging-in-Publication Data

The Deutero-Pauline letters : Ephesians, Colossians, 2 Thessalonians,
   1–2 Timothy, Titus / J. Paul Sampley . . . [et al.]. — Rev. ed. /
  Gerhard Krodel, editor.
     p.   cm. — (Proclamation commentaries)
    Rev. ed. of: Ephesians, Colossians, 2 Thessalonians, the Pastoral
  Epistles. c1978.
    Includes bibliographical references and index.
    ISBN 0-8006-2802-0 (alk. paper) :
    1. Bible. N.T. Ephesians—Criticism, interpretation, etc.
  2. Bible. N.T. Colossians—Criticism, interpretation, etc.
  3. Bible. N.T. Thessalonians—Criticism, interpretation, etc.
  4. Bible. N.T. Pastoral Epistles—Criticism, interpretation, etc.
  I. Sampley, J. Paul. II. Krodel, Gerhard, 1926–
  III. Ephesians, Colossians, 2 Thessalonians, the Pastoral Epistles.
  IV. Series.
  BS2650.2.D485   1993
  227—dc20
                                     93-31816
                                        CIP

Manufactured in the U.S.A.   AF 1-2802

97   96   95   94   93   1   2   3   4   5   6   7   8   9   10

CONTENTS

EDITOR'S FOREWORD

The letters discussed in this book bear Paul's name, although there is widespread agreement that they were written by his associates or followers under his name. Thus they give evidence of Paul's influence in the generation that followed him. The apostle Paul was not only the outstanding missionary-theologian during the first three decades of the church's existence—the one whose life's work was crowned by martyrdom—he was also a controversial figure, plagued by opposition even within churches he established (cf. Gal. 3:1; 5:12; 2 Cor. 11:13). His students and those who followed in his tradition endeavored to preserve his image and his legacy, and in the process they also struggled with each other. Different portraits of Paul emerge in the generation after him.

The author of Acts, for instance, presented Paul not only as a pious Jew (Acts 16:1-3; 20:16; 21:22-26; 23:6) but as unembroiled by controversies with other Christian leaders. In Acts, Paul agrees with the Apostles' Decree and introduces it into his churches (16:4), and he agrees with the advice of James (21:22-24). He was neither a renegade Jew nor a maverick apostle, as some later Jewish Christians portrayed him. Indeed, according to Acts, he was not an apostle on par with the Twelve, contrary to Paul's own claim (cf. Gal. 1:1).

The author of the Pastoral Epistles also portrayed a domesticated Paul who advocated the process of the institutionalization of the church and its accommodation with some of society's values. The latter can be seen most clearly in the new perspective on the place of women in the church that the Pastoral Epistles introduce (2 Tim. 2:8-15).

The author of 2 Thessalonians gives an insight into struggles among some of Paul's followers about the right eschatology. For some apocalyptically oriented Paulinists "the day of the Lord" was already present; they based their position on a prophetic oracle, on oral teaching, and on a letter bearing Paul's name (2 Thess. 2:2-3). The author of 2 Thessalonians denied having written such a letter, and he presented an apocalyptic timetable as Paul's original teaching (2 Thess. 2:5, 15).

Although the author of 2 Thessalonians as well as his opponents made use of apocalyptic traditions, other Paulinists, drawing on distinctly different traditions, held that the resurrection of believers had already taken place (2 Tim. 2:18). Their position found support in the bold declaration of Ephesians that in baptism God has "raised us up with him [Christ] and seated us with him in the heavenly places" (Eph. 2:6). Ephesians still affirms a future consummation (e.g., 5:25). But it is the distant future that Ephesians and the other Deutero-Pauline letters envision. Spatial categories have taken center stage in Ephesians as well as in Colossians, with which the author of Ephesians was familiar.

The need to speak the word in uncharted situations, to set boundaries over against falsehoods, to present Christian identity and conduct anew, to establish basic institutional structures for the church's life, and to locate Christian households within society in a manner that would deflect the reproach that Christianity undermined the basic unit of society—these were main concerns that prompted Paul's students to write letters in his name. Each of the Deutero-Pauline letters shifted Paul's theological emphases into new directions, and all were conscious of the authority of the apostle to the Gentiles and of apostolic traditions.

The reader who would like to pursue the phenomenon of pseudonymity in early Christian literature may turn to works such as: K. Aland, "The Problem of Anonymity and Pseudonymity in Christian Literature of the First Two Centuries," in *Authorship and Integrity of the New Testament*, Theological Collections 4 (London: SPCK, 1965), 1–13; D. G. Meade: *Pseudonymity and Canon*, WUNT 39 (Tübingen: Mohr-Siebeck, 1986; and Grand Rapids: Eerdmans, 1987); B. M. Metzger, "Literary Forgeries and Canonical Pseudepigrapha," *JBL* 91 (1972): 3–24; idem, *New Testament Studies*, NTTS 10 (Leiden: Brill, 1980); K. M. Fischer, "Amerkungen zur Pseudepigraphie im Neuen Testament," *NTS* 23, (1976): 76–81; N. Brox, *Pseudepigraphie in der heidnischen und jüdisch-christlichen Antike* (Darmstadt: Wissenschaftliche Buchgesellschaft, 1977); M. Wolter, "Die anonymen Schriften des Neuen Testaments: Annäherungsversuch an ein literarisches Phänomen," *ZNW* 79 (1988): 1–16.

J. Paul Sampley is Professor of New Testament at the School of Theology, Boston University, Boston, Mass.; Arland J. Hultgren is Professor of New Testament, Luther Northwestern Theological Seminary, St. Paul, Minn.; Walter Taylor is Professor of New Testament, Trinity Lutheran Seminary, Columbus, Ohio.

Gerhard Krodel
Professor of New Testament
Lutheran Theological Seminary,
Gettysburg, Pennsylvania

ABBREVIATIONS

AB	Anchor Bible
AnBib	Analecta Biblica
AV	Authorized (King James) Version
BAGD	W. Bauer, W. F. Arndt, W. F. Gingrich, and F. W. Danker, *Greek-English Lexicon of the New Testament*
BJRL	*Bulletin of the John Rylands University Library of Manchester*
CBQ	*Catholic Biblical Quarterly*
CurTM	*Currents in Theology and Mission*
EKKNT	Evangelisch-katholischer Kommentar zum Neuen Testament
ETS	Erfurter theologische Studien
ExpTim	*Expository Times*
FRLANT	Forschungen zur Religion und Literatur des Alten und Neuen Testaments
HNTC	Harper's New Testament Commentaries
HUT	Hermeneutische Untersuchungen zur Theologie
ICC	International Critical Commentary
IDBSup	*Interpreter's Dictionary of the Bible, Supplementary Volume*
JBL	*Journal of Biblical Literature*
JSNT	*Journal for the Study of the New Testament*
JSNTSup	Journal for the Study of the New Testament—Supplement Series
LXX	Septuagint
MNTC	Moffat's New Testament Commentary
NCBC	New Century Bible Commentary
NICNT	New International Commentary on the New Testament
NIGTC	New International Greek Testament Commentary
NIV	New International Version
NovTSup	Novum Testamentum, Supplements
NRSV	New Revised Standard Version
NTD	Das Neue Testament Deutsch
NTS	*New Testament Studies*
NTTS	New Testament Tools and Studies

RevExp	*Review and Expositor*
RNT	Regensburger Neues Testament
RSV	Revised Standard Version
SBLDS	Society of Biblical Literature Dissertation Series
SBLMS	Society of Biblical Literature Monograph Series
SBLSBS	Society of Biblical Literature Sources for Biblical Study
SBT	Studies in Biblical Theology
SNTSMS	Society for New Testament Study Monograph Series
SUNT	Studien zur Umwelt des Neuen Testaments
TDNT	G. Kittel and G. Friedrich, eds., *Theological Dictionary of the New Testament*
THKNT	Theologischer Handkommentar zum Neuen Testament
TQ	*Theologische Quartalschrift*
WBC	Word Biblical Commentary
WUNT	Wissenschaftliche Untersuchungen zum Neuen Testament
ZNW	*Zeitschrift für die neutestamentliche Wissenschaft*

EPHESIANS

Introduction

The document entitled "The Letter of Paul to the Ephesians" is an enigma on several counts. First, according to the best Greek manuscripts the actual text of the letter does not identify any specific destination. We know the document by its superscription—"The Letter of Paul to the Ephesians"— but the superscriptions of the NT documents were added late in the second century. The best Greek manuscripts for this document simply open: "Paul . . . to the saints who are also faithful in Christ Jesus" (1:1). One of Paul's earliest interpreters, the second-century heretic Marcion, thought this letter might be the otherwise lost "letter to the Laodiceans" mentioned in Col. 4:16. We simply do not know for whom the letter was intended, but for convenience I take the name "Ephesians" to refer both to the document and to its recipients.

We also cannot be sure exactly why it was written. Paul's letters usually respond to a crisis or a problem, to some discernible and specific historical situation. Even Romans, sent to churches that Paul's preaching did not establish, has identifiable reasons for being written: It is an apostolic response to ethnic problems in those churches, and it is a "bread-and-butter" letter written in advance of his arrival, seeking support for his mission to Spain (cf. 15:22-24). Ephesians, however, lacks clues concerning a concrete crisis or occasion. Admonitions for unity are scattered through the letter (cf. esp. 4:1-16), but if there was a threat to unity among the recipients, the clues are too general to reconstruct the specifics. In 2:11-20 the author asserts that Jews and Gentiles have been brought together in Christ; was there fear of a Jewish-Gentile split among the believers for whom this letter was intended? Not obviously. In fact, the recipients are identified as Gentiles (2:1; 3:2); the author reaffirms that Gentiles have become a part of the "commonwealth of Israel" (2:12), but the declaration is more a reminder than news. In sum, therefore, the Letter to the Ephesians is of a very general character. The precise historical purposes of its author are hidden from the modern reader. Nevertheless, Ephesians became a widely quoted and appreciated letter among church leaders in the second century and has remained so down through history.

Although we have no decisive answers to the questions to whom this letter was written and for what purpose it was drafted, the question of authorship seems less problematic at first glance. The letter directly identifies Paul as its author: "Paul, an apostle of Christ Jesus by the will of God" (1:1). Until Erasmus, the great sixteenth-century scholar, that assignation was unquestioned: It was Paul who wrote Ephesians. Erasmus noted such stylistic differences, however, that he concluded Ephesians was written by someone besides the Paul of the other letters. From Erasmus's time to the present, the question has been debated, and no doubt will continue to be because the issue is not decisively demonstrable one way or the other. Whatever one's decision on the authorship of Ephesians, it must be made in comparison with the undisputed Pauline letters—Romans, 1 and 2 Corinthians, Galatians, Philippians, 1 Thessalonians, and Philemon—and in conjunction with Colossians, the letter to which it has the greatest affinities and about which strong questions can also be raised as to its Pauline authorship.

Because the letter declares itself Pauline, the burden of proof lies with those who would question its explicit claim. The problems with Pauline attribution of Ephesians revolve around the following issues: (1) peculiar style and vocabulary; and (2) distinctive assertions or viewpoint.

Peculiar Style and Vocabulary

The student of the Greek text is immediately struck by Ephesians' complex, long sentences, a common feature in Ephesians but relatively infrequent in the undisputed Pauline letters. Like delicate and complicated filigrees, Ephesians' sentences are composed of appositional phrases, genitival constructions, and relative clauses interwoven with one another and hanging from one or two central verbs. Ephesians 1:15-23 is one such example; here the NRSV translators have preserved the sentence intact, though that is not always their pattern (cf. 1:3-14; 4:11-16).

The vocabulary of Ephesians seems strange in two ways. First, Ephesians contains a fair number of words that, though they are entirely missing from the undisputed Pauline letters, are found frequently in the later NT writings and in the early church fathers. Examples are such terms as "commonwealth" *(politeia,* 2:11; cf. *politeuma* in Phil. 3:20), "likeness" *(hosiotēs,* 4:24), "debauchery" *(asōtia,* 5:18), and "be tossed here and there by waves" *(klydōnizomai,* 4:14).

But the vocabulary of Ephesians is distinctive on another count as well. The author of Ephesians may employ a term different from the one that might be expected on the basis of the unquestioned Pauline correspondence, or he may introduce terms not represented in the other letters. A noticeable example of the former is his tendency to use "heavenly places" *(ta epour-aniois,* 1:3, 20; 2:6; 3:10; 6:12) where Paul generally refers to "heaven" *(ouranos;* cf., e.g., Rom. 1:18; Gal. 1:8; Phil. 3:20; but contrast 1 Cor. 15:40, 48, 49). As an example of terms not present in the other letters, consider the designation of Christ as "the Beloved" *(ho ēgapēmenos,* 1:6) or the use of the Semitic "blood and flesh" as a euphemism for "people" (6:12).

Distinctive Assertions and Viewpoint

Style and vocabulary aside, more weighty objections to the Pauline authorship of Ephesians center on some of the assertions made in that letter. Perhaps most striking is the shift in emphasis from predominantly temporal categories in the indisputably authentic letters (cf. Rom. 13:11-12; 1 Cor. 7:26, 29, 31; 15:51-52; 2 Cor. 4:17; 1 Thess. 4:13) to an emphasis on spatial conceptions (Eph. 1:20; 2:6), perhaps as a way of dealing with the delay of Christ's return. Related is another set of distinctive claims in Ephesians: believers already share in Christ's resurrection (God "made us alive together with Christ . . . and raised us up with him, and seated us with him in the heavenly places," 2:5-6); they have already been saved (2:5, 8). In the seven undisputed letters Paul is careful to affirm that both being raised with Christ and salvation are future for the believers, but more on this topic later.

Some find other claims in Ephesians difficult to reconcile with the indisputably authentic Pauline letters. How, for example, does the view of marriage set forward in Eph. 5:22-33, where the husband and the wife are paralleled with Christ and the church, fit with Paul's stated preference that people not marry and with his claim that marriage is a last resort, as an outlet for otherwise uncontrollable sexual drives (1 Cor. 7:8-9, 32-38)? Likewise, for the unquestioned Pauline letters, sin is a power and justification is the means of escaping its clutch (Rom. 5:6-11; 7:8, 11), but Ephesians has *sins,* trespasses, and their forgiveness (1:7; 2:1; 4:32). For one other example, in Ephesians the Pauline "church in your house" (Philem. 2) is portrayed as having a cosmic function (Eph. 3:10) and Christ is its head (1:21-22; 4:15; 5:23), an extension of the image from its portrayal in Rom. 12:4-5 and 1 Cor. 12:12-26.

These are some of the problems that interpreters have found with affirming Pauline authorship of Ephesians. Although the case for or against Pauline authorship of Ephesians falls short of proof, the problems seem to outweigh the similarities. Accordingly, I proceed on the assumption that Paul did not write Ephesians. It was very likely composed by a close follower of Paul who, making Paul present across time, wrote this letter to some gentile Christians, on behalf of Paul, to call them back to the basics of their faith and to instruct them further on how to live properly before God and with other believers. Now I turn to the letter itself.

God's Plan and the Believer's Place in It

God has a plan that is being realized. The clear message to the readers is that they have a secure place in God's unfolding purpose. Different terms describe the plan: It is a "mystery" *(mystērion,* 1:9), a "purpose" *(eudokian,* 1:9), a "counsel" *(boulē,* 1:11), a "plan" *(oikonomia,* 3:9). This plan, though it was shrouded in mystery in the past so that it has not been known by "former generations" (3:5; cf. 3:9), was operative in the past. The plan is not an innovation; God has prepared it beforehand. The key is this: The eternal purpose of God, hidden for ages, has come to a climax in Christ Jesus. What was hidden is now disclosed. Furthermore, those who are "in Christ," those who believe, can now see their place in God's plan and are instructed concerning how to coordinate their lives with God's purpose. Moreover, their inclusion in this grand plan is sealed by the "promised Holy Spirit" (1:13).

Two overriding purposes dominate the first half of the letter (chaps. 1–3): The faithful are assured of their secure place in God's purposes and are instructed concerning the consequences of this election. Throughout the opening chapters, the aorist, the tense of completed action in the past, prevails. The situation of the readers is *already* secured. God's action in Christ has made sure of that. God "has blessed us" (1:3). God "chose us" (1:4) and "destined us" (1:5). "We have redemption" (1:7). "You . . . were marked with the seal of the promised Holy Spirit" (1:13) and therefore already have the down payment (1:14) of what is to come. This all reads as if it were reminders of what the readers are expected to know; it rings more of reprise than of first explanation.

A comparison with the unquestionably Pauline letters shows Ephesians' eagerness to clarify what has already been accomplished for the believers. Ephesians declares that God "made us alive together with Christ . . . and raised us up with him" (2:5-6). Already alive together with Christ; already raised with him! In Philippians Paul is more guarded: "becoming like him in his death, if somehow I may attain the resurrection from the dead" (Phil. 3:10-11). There Paul does not question the believer's solidarity with Christ in his *death,* but sharing his resurrection is still a hope for the future. Romans 6:5 makes the same temporal distinction found in Philippians: "For if we have been united with him in a death like his, we will certainly be united with him in a resurrection like his." With Ephesians, however, the distinction collapses: The believers share with Christ not only his death but also his resurrection. The same point can be made with regard to salvation. Ephesians claims that believers have salvation: "by grace you have been saved" (2:5, 8). For Paul, believers already have justification or reconciliation; they do not yet have salvation because salvation belongs to the end-time finishing-up work of God (Rom. 5:6-11). Ephesians clearly stresses the completeness and the fullness of God's action in Christ and the abundance of God's riches made available to the believers.

Because of the immeasurable riches of God's grace, the readers are now caught up in God's plan and they are asked to remember their baptism in which each of them was given a "new self, created according to the likeness of God" (Eph. 4:24). The believers are not what they used to be but are new creatures by God's grace. Ephesians sheds light on the new situation of the believers by contrasting their life apart from faith. They are no longer "aliens" and "strangers . . . having no hope and without God" (2:12). They are no longer "dead through the trespasses and sins in which you once walked" (2:1-2, RSV). "No longer walk as the Gentiles walk, in the futility of their minds" (4:17, my trans.). Although the metaphor shifts, the same point is made: "Once you were darkness, but now you are light in the Lord; walk as children of light" (5:8, RSV). The last statement—"walk as children of light"—shows that the author's purpose is not one of simple contrast; rather he is eager to remind and to instruct them concerning the life that is appropriate to their new status. Believers must now "walk" differently from before.

The Proper "Walk"

While the opening half of Ephesians (chaps. 1–3) describes God's now-revealed plan and reminds the believers of their place in it, the second half of the letter (chaps. 4–6) instructs the readers concerning the "walk," the way of life, that is appropriate to the plan now under way in Christ. The theme that binds chapters 4–6 together is the "proper walk."

For Jews and Gentiles in Jesus' time, "walk" was a common metaphor for the way one lived. To walk a certain way was to live in that manner. When one's situation changed, one walked or behaved differently. The recipients of Ephesians undersood well the appeal in the second half of the letter to "walk worthy of the calling," or as the NRSV has translated it, "lead a life worthy of the calling" (4:1).

Like most of the undisputed Pauline letters, so also Ephesians moves toward an appeal section that depicts appropriate behavior. A classic example is Rom. 12:1: "I appeal to you therefore, brothers and sisters, by the mercies of God, to present your bodies as a living sacrifice, holy and acceptable to God." Ephesians follows the same pattern: "I appeal to you, therefore, I the prisoner in the Lord, that you walk in a manner worthy of the calling to which you have been called" (4:1, my trans.). To walk "worthy" suggests that there is a walk that is "unworthy," inappropriate.

And sure enough, when the theme of walking next appears in Ephesians, the author says: "you must no longer walk as the Gentiles walk" (4:17, my trans.).

The theme of the proper walk punctuates chapter 5 as well. The chapter opens with the admonition to walk in love (5:2), and its instructions are bracketed with a reprise of the same theme cast in a sweeping form: "Watch carefully then how you walk" (5:15, my trans.; cf. also 5:8).

So in Ephesians, the readers are reminded of God's formerly hidden but now disclosed plan in which they have a particular place and part. By the commonplace idea of life as a walk the author schools the readers concerning how God's purpose and plan impinge on the way they comport their lives. In sum, the particulars of the Letter to the Ephesians must be seen against the backdrop provided by these fundamental claims: God's plan, though formerly hidden, is now not only disclosed but under way. The believers understand this plan and know themselves to be included in it by God's grace. Accordingly, they must walk in a way appropriate to God's plan and their place in it. I turn next to an examination of some special features of the letter.

The Varied Images of the Church in Ephesians

Across the centuries readers of Ephesians have been struck by its conception of the church. Like the Pauline letters (cf. 1 Cor. 1:2), Ephesians knows that it is "the saints who are also faithful in Christ Jesus" (1:1, RSV) who are brought together into community with one another as a result of "the immeasurable riches of his grace in kindness toward us in Christ Jesus" (2:7). The church is composed of all the "saints," that is, of those set apart for God. They are "members of the household of God" (2:19).

Ephesians' view of the church, though, may be seen more distinctly by means of a comparison with Paul. Paul's use of the term "church" is very localized. For him the word "church" never functions collectively to tie believers who live in one place with those who live in another. In Paul's undisputed letters, "church" signifies the worshiping believers who gather together in one place. For example, they may be "the church in your house" (Philem. 2) or they may be groups of believers scattered across the Roman province of Galatia and addressed as "the *churches* of Galatia" (Gal. 1:2).

In Ephesians we no longer encounter a localized use of the term "church," a fact that becomes clear the first time the word appears. Eager to stress what has already been accomplished in Christ, the author of Ephesians sets up the universe, the cosmos, as the only vista against which the truly massive proportions of God's plan can be appreciated. Christ has been raised by God and made to sit "at his right hand in the heavenly places" (1:20). That position insures his predominance over "all rule and authority and power and dominion" (1:21). The same point is reaffirmed in the next verse by utilizing the language of the Psalms: God "has put all things under his [Christ's] feet" (1:22; cf. Ps. 110:1). The mention of "feet" triggers the fertile mind of the author to make the same assertion again, this time using the metaphor of "head": God "has made him [Christ] the head over all things for the church" (Eph. 1:22). The first explicit mention of the church in Ephesians, therefore, comes in a context where the author portrays the cosmic significance of God's action in Christ. God has raised Christ to power in the heavenly places, far above all rival and contending powers, and all of this bears directly on the church. The dominion over all things granted by God to Christ has the church as its object. God's plan is cosmic and the church fits in that plan.

As the letter unfolds, the picture is confirmed. The church is the beneficiary of God's cosmic plan and the church has a task appropriate to that plan. The "God who created all things" now discloses "what is the plan of the mystery hidden for ages" (3:9), namely, "that through the church the wisdom of God in its rich variety might now be made known to the rulers and authorities in the heavenly places" (3:10). God's purpose is unfolding *for* the church (it is the beneficiary) and *through* the church (it is the agent by which the plan is disclosed). The church's task is on a scale with God's purpose, of which it is so directly a part. As the plan is cosmic in proportions, so is the church. The church that Ephesians describes is therefore not simply the localized gathering of worshiping believers who meet in someone's home. It includes those persons but views them on a grander scale as the agents who disclose God's purpose—even in the heavenly places (3:10). Accordingly, the plural, "churches," would be absolutely inappropriate to Ephesians and is never found there.

Baptism is a fundamental link of the readers to the church and to God's plan. Although the term "baptism" is explicitly mentioned only once (4:5), the imagery and terminology of baptism are powerfully present. In some traditions, early Christian baptism employed a symbolic divestment and rerobing as well as some rather set formulas that might be spoken (cf. Gal. 3:28). The author of Ephesians draws richly upon such symbolism when he writes of "putting away," that is, taking off (4:22, 25, 31), and "putting on" or "clothing" (4:24; 6:11, 14). Similarly the marking "with the seal of the promised Holy Spirit" (1:13; 4:30) probably provides another link to baptism. The language of vestment associated with baptism provides Ephesians with a means of describing what the believers have taken off as they have discarded their former life: "your old self" (4:22), "falsehood" (4:25), "all bitterness and wrath and anger and wrangling and slander, together with all malice" (4:31). Believers are newly clothed with a "new self" (4:24), with the "breastplate of righteousness" (6:14), the "whole armor of God" (6:11), and "whatever will make you ready to proclaim the gospel of peace" (6:15). In all of this, baptism is not viewed as a ritual relegated to the beginning of the life of faith. On the contrary, baptism provides the foundation for life, for participation in God's plan, and for guidance in daily conduct. Indeed, Ephesians' view of life in the church and in the world is so tied with baptism that some scholars have thought that the document might reflect some instruction for newly baptized persons.

Against the vista provided by the cosmic backdrop of God's unfolding plan for and through the church, the author of Ephesians develops a rich view of the church through his creative use of various images and metaphors. A brief examination of the primary images of the church helps disclose the multifaceted portrait Ephesians offers.

The Body of Christ

The "body of Christ" is Ephesians' best-known and most pervasive metaphor for the church. Beginning with 1:22 the church is directly identified as the "body of Christ," and the motif continues through most of the letter.

As a way of assessing the prominence of this image in Ephesians, one may observe that the indisputably authentic Pauline letters do not frequently resort to this image. Among the Pauline letters only Romans 12 and 1 Corinthians 12 feature the metaphor (cf. Rom. 7:4; 1 Cor. 10:16), and in both cases they introduce it in the interest of reaffirming Christian unity.

In Ephesians, however, the "body of Christ" image is used sweepingly across the document and serves four major functions. First, and basically, it allows the author to explain how the believers relate to Christ. As with the unquestioned Pauline letters, so in Ephesians the believers are "in Christ." Ephesians uses the "body of Christ" terminology to declare and develop that central Pauline claim. As a result, the closely related phrases "in Christ" and "in the body of Christ" are used interchangeably (cf. 2:15-16). The author of Ephesians apparently assumes that his readers already understand this point and do not need to be convinced. Nowhere does he try to persuade them of its truth; rather, the claim that "we are members of his body" (5:30) is made in so matter-of-fact fashion that it is a fixed point from which the author reasons. The "body of Christ" terminology in Ephesians helps the author develop for his readers the implications of their being "in Christ." They are members of Christ's body.

Second, the "body of Christ" image helps the author express the way that individual believers belong to one another and should relate to one another. As a body has many members (cf. 1 Cor. 12:12), it follows that the different members of the same body are members of one another (Eph.

4:25). Accordingly, the believers are to live together in unity. Like any healthy body, the different members ought to build up one another. Love is the means. The body of Christ upbuilds itself in love (4:16). When there is unity and when the diverse gifts of Christ are functioning as they should, the body of Christ is edified (4:12).

The author of Ephesians extends the metaphor and develops the same point. When all the members are functioning together as they should, when the different gifts are operative, the body of Christ is built up until all attain "to maturity, to the measure of the full stature of Christ" (4:13). A construction metaphor, "edification," gives way to an image of growth, but the point is the same. When properly in unity, the body of Christ grows, is built up (4:15-16).

In these two functions of the "body of Christ" terminology—to illuminate how believers are related to Christ and how believers belong to each other— Ephesians is very much in line with the use of the image in 1 Corinthians 12 and in Romans 12. But a third way that Ephesians employs the "body of Christ" image is found nowhere in the undisputed Pauline letters. According to Ephesians, not only are the faithful members of Christ's body members of the church, but Christ is the "head" of that body, the church. Believers are "in Christ" and at the same time enjoined to "grow up in every way into him who is the head, into Christ" (4:15). As head of his body, the church, Christ is the goal toward which the growth of the body must aspire. The author also turns the matter around: Christ, the head, is also the *source* of the power that enables bodily growth, because from that head "the whole body, joined and knit together by every ligament with which it is equipped, as each part is working properly, promotes the body's growth in building itself up in love" (4:16). When the church as the body of Christ recognizes Christ, its head, as its goal (4:15) and its source (4:16), then bodily growth and edification take place.

Implicit in this notion of Christ as head of his body, the church, is a necessary submission of the body to the head. In this regard, what is implicit through much of the letter is directly expressed in the household code addressed to wives (5:22-24). There wives are urged to be submissive to their husbands "as to the Lord" (5:22). The rationale for such submission is found in the analogies or parallels the author sees between the wife's relation to the husband and the church's relation to Christ. "For the husband is the head of the wife as Christ is the head of the church, his body" (5:23, RSV). The church must be submissive to its Lord, its head.

In sum, the author of Ephesians capitalizes on the image of the head in three complementary ways: the head, Christ, is the goal toward which the body, the church, should live; the head is the source by which the body may achieve growth; and the head is Lord over the body and consequently the body, the church, must be submissive to Christ.

The fourth major function of the "body of Christ" image in Ephesians is to help the faithful understand their place in the universe, the cosmos. The "body of Christ" terminology is first introduced near the conclusion of the heavily christological section 1:3-23, whose core affirmations are that God "has put all things under his [Christ's] feet and has made him the head over all things for the church, which is his body" (1:22-23). The church as the body of Christ has a special place in God's plan for all of creation, for the universe. Accordingly, the church has a role in the cosmic lordship of Christ over all things.

Ephesians' "body" language was common coinage in the Greco-Roman world and would have been readily understood by the Gentiles to whom Ephesians is apparently directed. For example, the Stoics made considerable use of the "body" metaphor as a way of describing social groupings. The people in the social group were the members of the body. Even the universe could be viewed as a body, an organic whole, with each person understood as a member of that body. Under the Roman emperor Nero (A.D. 54–68), the empire was referred to as Nero's body, and in some ways like Ephesians, Nero was said to be the head of his body, the empire. Ephesians' use of the terminology is not peculiar when viewed against the background of the Greco-Roman world, but rather provides a readily understandable means for the author to convey important points about Christ and the church to his gentile audience.

The Bride of Christ

The early churches cherished the image of the church as the bride to Christ, the groom. Jesus' sayings mention bridal banquets (Luke 14:8-14; Matt. 22:1-14) and bridegrooms (Matt. 25:1-13), and some sayings even seem to identify Christ as the bridegroom (Mark 2:19-20; Matt. 9:15; Luke 5:34-35). In 2 Corinthians Paul refers to himself as what we might call the best man or matchmaker who has prepared the church as the bride for Christ (11:2). But the image is developed in the NT only in the book of Revelation (19:6-10) and Eph. 5:21-33.

The idea of a divine marriage is certainly not the invention of the early church; nor is it even a construction of ancient Israel, although the Israelites certainly knew about it. It is an archaic image present in the oldest evidence from the ancient Near East, where the conviction was that gods and goddesses formed marriages; such stories helped people understand their own origins and relationship to the deities. From such a past, Israel inherited the notion and applied it at several points in the prophetic literature to Israel and Yahweh, her God. Ezekiel speaks of the youngster that Yahweh found in the wilderness and nursed into a beautiful maiden whom he took for his wife (Ezekiel 16). The young woman is identified as Jerusalem (16:3), representing Israel. Ezekiel tells the story so that he can report on her subsequent whoring after others, that is, her unfaithfulness to Yahweh (16:15-34). Hosea picks up much the same idea, although he devotes no time to Israel's youth. He moves directly to portray Israel as Yahweh's unfaithful wife (Hosea 2–3). Elsewhere in Israel's traditions, the Song of Songs is replete with the language of two lovers committed to each other, material that by rabbinic times was understood allegorically of Yahweh and Israel. That rich mine of images lay open before the early Christians in the very Scriptures they shared with Israel. It is not surprising that the Christians took over the imagery and with slight modification applied it to Christ and the church.

Ephesians shares with most of the older divine-marriage accounts three identifiable traits or emphases: (1) the bride must be free of all blemishes and defects because they would detract from her beauty; (2) she must have a dowry, and she is clothed in that dowry so that she is resplendent; and (3) she must appear before the groom, prepared for the consummation of the marriage.

Ephesians recognizes that the cleansing and purifying of the church as Christ's bride has taken place because of Christ's love and death for her: "Christ loved the church and gave himself up for her, in order to make her holy by cleansing her with the washing of water by the word" (5:25-26). Accordingly, she is without blemish or defect that would diminish her splendor. Not only did he purify her—in Ephesians, that is an action completed in the past—but Christ continues in the present to nourish and care for her: "For no one ever hates his own body, but he nourishes and tenderly cares for it, just as Christ does for the church" (5:29).

What was done in the past, the cleansing, the purifying by Christ's death, establishes the church in the present when she is nourished and cherished by Christ, and leads toward an event in the distant future. All that has been done for the church and all that is currently being done for her point to the great moment in the future when the bride, properly cleansed and endowed with purity, will be presented to Christ. The anticipated consummation of marriage is tantamount to judgment. "Christ loved the church and gave himself up for her . . . so as to present the church to himself in splendor, without a spot or wrinkle or anything of the kind" (5:25-27). What is the church's dowry as she stands before Christ? Her splendor of purity and holiness. Stated in negatives, it is her being without blemish, without spot, wrinkle, or any such thing that might detract from that holiness.

The concern with holiness and purity of the bride touches on a larger theme in Ephesians. From the beginning the letter has sounded this note: the readers have been chosen "before the foundation of the world" (1:4), and they are moving toward the judgment-presentation of the bride before the groom. From before all time until the end of time—these are the borders of God's purposes with the faithful. God "chose us in Christ before the foundation of the world to be holy and blameless before him" (1:4). The word translated "blameless" *(amōmos,* literally, "without blemish") is the same term that appears, again linked with "holy," in the passage that anticipates the presentation of the bride before Christ: "so that she may be holy and without blemish *[amōmos]"* (5:27). Although the term translated "without blemish" occurs in Ephesians only in 1:4 and 5:27, the related and positively stated concern with holiness is a strong motif throughout the letter (1:1, 4, 13, 15, 18; 2:19, 21; 3:5, 8, 18; 4:12, 30; 5:3, 27; 6:18). In Ephesians, as in the Pauline letters, to be "holy" or a "saint"— the Greek word *(hagios)* is the same for both—is to be set apart for God on the basis of God's initiative, and is associated with Ephesians' strong interest in baptism noted earlier. It is God who makes saints by the free gift of grace and love.

In these verses portraying the church as the bride of Christ (5:22-33), the concern with blemishes merits one more observation. Deep-seated in the Scriptures of Israel are extensive regulations concerning the condition of the creatures to be offered in sacrifice to God. These guidelines prohibited anyone from sacrificing a lame, sick, or otherwise decrepit animal under the guise of fulfilling one's obligations to God. The code word that recurs in these injunctions is "blemish"; the animals must be without blemish of any kind. At some point in Israel's life, the concern with blemishes was imposed as a standard by which to judge the purity expected of priests (Lev. 21:17-23). The author of Ephesians embraces this pervasive concern for purity and applies it to the church as Christ's bride (cf. Deut. 24:1). The church, purified in baptism, is to be presented to Christ as his pure bride. The ancient divine-marriage idea demands that the bride be presented in splendor. Ephesians defines that splendor positively, "holy," and negatively, "without blemish." Together the two terms, "holy" and "without blemish," mirror the author's pervasive concern for the church. The church must live in the holiness granted in baptism by God's grace; the church must walk in such a way that it avoids any blemishes that would mar her God-bestowed purity.

The author of Ephesians has chosen a striking point at which to introduce the "bride of Christ" metaphor. It appears in the opening set of addresses to husbands and wives in the household code (5:21—6:9). The sacred marriage of Christ and the church is carefully interwoven with the author's admonitions to the wife and the husband. Human marriage has been raised to lofty heights by the very association, though many of us may feel uneasy with some features of the author's submissive portrait of the wife's role. Nevertheless, the author's point is that the core of the family or household is the husband and wife and that when they live in proper relation to one another they mirror God's larger plans and purposes. Indeed, one should put it even more directly: When husband and wife relate as they should, they make real in the human family God's cosmic purposes in Christ. No wonder the author of Ephesians can tell his readers they were formerly homeless but now are members of the household of God (2:19)!

The Household of God

When Ephesians was written, the basic sociological unit was not simply composed of two parents and their offspring. Instead, the fundamental social organization was the household, which comprised not only the parents and children but also slaves. The web of relationships in such a household included not only husbands/wives, parents/children, and children/children but also the relation of slaves to the rest of these people. Also resident might be other relatives and persons plying the same trade as those of the household. The author of Ephesians employs "household" and "family" as interchangeable social metaphors to describe the new situation in which believers find themselves. Under God the Father, the faithful have become "beloved children" (5:1), "children of light" (5:8). Indeed, they are described in the beginning of the letter as God's adopted "children" (1:5). The believers have been born into a new life, a new family (3:14). As the author puts it succinctly, they are "members of the household of God" (2:19).

The analogy is extended. Just as the children of human families can hope for a legacy, so the new children of God can anticipate an inheritance. There is one difference: the inheritance from God is so lavish that it strains the language as the author tries to give it adequate expression. Nearly redundant phrases result: "riches . . . lavished on us" (1:7-8), "the riches of his glorious inheritance" (1:18), and "immeasurable riches" (2:7).

The unity of the new family of God also finds expression through the metaphor of inheritance. The "mystery of Christ" (3:4) is disclosed: "Gentiles have become fellow heirs" (3:6). The inheritance is open to all who are included in God's new family, whether they be Jews or Gentiles. There can be no distinction between Jew and Gentile when God is the Father and expresses care over all families by giving them names (3:14). God's power expresses itself across as vast and inclusive a scope as the mind can imagine—on earth and in heaven—to name all families and thereby to bring them together under him as Father. God is the Father of the faithful; the believers should live as the beloved children that they have become in Christ. As such they can be confident of their ultimate sharing in the great riches that make up their inheritance.

Ephesians' pervasive employment of the image of father is a reflection of the author's social environment where the paterfamilias had the legal and social responsibility for the care and protection of his family. With that responsibility went power and authority. In the author's effort to express God's great and powerful love directed toward the faithful, the image of father of the household is depicted on a cosmic scale.

As Ephesians contrasts two ways of walking, so in terminology appropriate to the household it has rival notions of childhood. The author reminds the readers that they "were children of wrath, like everyone else" (2:3; cf. 4:14). Believers are no longer to associate with (literally) the "sons of disobedience," a Semitic way of saying "those who are disobedient" (5:6; cf. 2:2). Once the readers were the wrong type of children; now they are properly children of God.

In terms akin to those employed in the Dead Sea Scrolls, the author sets the proper childhood over against the errant one. "For once you were darkness, but now in the Lord you are light. Live [Greek: 'walk'] as children of light" (5:8). Once more the metaphor of the walk is intertwined with being proper children: "Therefore become imitators of God, as beloved children, and walk in love" (5:1-2, my trans.).

So there are two walks, two childhoods. The readers who walk as they should are living as children of light, as God's beloved children. The same understanding is expressed in another way: There are two spirits. Although the discussion of the rival spirits governing life is not developed at length in Ephesians, it is present. The readers are reminded that they once followed "the spirit that is now at work among those who are disobedient" (2:2), but they now find themselves under the guidance of a different spirit, the Holy Spirit. As believers in Christ, they have been "marked with the seal of the promised Holy Spirit; this is the pledge of our inheritance" (1:13-14).

The different spirits lead in different directions. The children who follow the spirit that governs disobedience are the children of wrath, children destined for wrath. The children who are sealed with the promised Holy Spirit have a radically different future. It includes an inheritance of incredible riches—and the promised Holy Spirit is the guarantee or down payment *(arrobōn)* of it (1:14). Thus the author contrasts rival "walks," rival "childhoods," and rival "spirits." The faithful, those true children who are sealed with the Holy Spirit and walk appropriately to their calling in Christ, are the ones who imitate God "as beloved children" (5:1) and walk in love (5:2) and aim for the inheritance proper to the true children of God. It is these faithful who make up the household of God.

Fellow Citizens with the Saints

In the world of the original readers of this letter, a larger social unit by which people normally identified themselves was the city, city-state *(polis)*, or province to which they belonged. Identity was in part disclosed by citizenship. Exile was one of the sterner penalties that could be imposed on an individual. The author of Ephesians casts this image on a large scale, describing the readers' prefaith situation as one of being strangers, sojourners, aliens, wanderers (2:19). They had been persons without citizenship.

To describe their new situation in Christ, however, the author deftly turns the image around and declares that the faithful are now "citizens with the saints" (2:19). Whereas before they were aliens, now they have citizenship, and the author uses a strong word, *sympolitai*, "joint-citizens" or "fellow citizens," to affirm that the readers are now citizens on full parity with the saints. In fact they too are saints, as the author directly addresses them in the opening verse of the letter. The church is peopled with saints. What does it mean to belong to this faithful community? It is to have a special citizenship, a saintly one, in God's *polis*, God's kingdom.

The church viewed as household and as a new citizenship are complementary pictures. Although drawing from different social contexts, the author uses both images to describe the new status of the faithful in Christ.

The Holy Temple

House metaphors and indeed construction images are well known in the Pauline correspondence (1 Cor. 3:10-15; cf. Rom. 15:20). In Ephesians the model of the "holy temple" emerges from a concatenation of images near the end of chapter 2. There proper citizenship merges into the notion of the household of God. The latter elicits the image of a building. The author of Ephesians uses that opportunity to describe nearly everything about this structure but the shape of the roof! What is the foundation? The prophets and apostles. The cornerstone? Christ Jesus. In Christ, "the whole structure is joined together and grows into a holy temple in the Lord" (2:21). Then, with somewhat cumbersome language, the author shows how the readers relate to that holy temple. In Christ they are built into the temple, "into a dwelling place for God" (2:22).

Apart from 2:21, Ephesians has no other explicit mention of the holy temple. There may be an indirect reference to it, however. As chapter 3 moves toward its powerful conclusion, the author reports his prayer for the faithful. Themes first related to "temple" at the end of chapter 2 reemerge near the end of chapter 3. The presence of the Spirit is important in both passages (2:22; 3:16). The temple as the "dwelling place for God" (2:22) is paralleled by the heart of the faithful as the dwelling place of Christ (3:17). The "foundation" of the holy temple is the prophets and apostles (2:20); later the author prays that the readers may have power because they are "rooted and grounded in love" (3:17; the term "grounded" here is the same as that for "foundation" in 2:20). One final point of possible connection: because the readers have their foundation properly established on love, the author prays that they "may have the power to comprehend, with all the saints, what is the breadth and length and height and depth" (3:18). But of what? What is it of which the readers are to know the measurements? From Numbers through Amos (7:7-8) through to the book of Revelation (11:1-2), a set of traditions endures that the temple—or at least Jerusalem—is measured or gauged. In Revelation the measuring of the temple and the altar and the people who worship there clearly suggests judgment. How does the temple measure up to its calling? It is possible here in Ephesians that the author's prayer portrays the believers as built on the proper foundation and accordingly knowing the parameters of their new dwelling.

One New Humanity in Place of the Two

In terms appropriate to Israel, 2:11 opens with an address to "you Gentiles," reminding the readers that they were "once aliens from the commonwealth of Israel, and strangers to the covenants of promise" (2:12). Borrowing further from Israel (cf. Isa. 57:19 and Zech. 6:15) the author describes how in Christ those "far off have been brought near" (2:13). The "dividing wall, that is, the hostility between us" (2:14) has been broken down. Both *(ta amphotera,* "the two")* have become one (2:14). Given the context, those "far off" and those "near" are intended; they have become one. For this author it is Gentiles and Jews who are made one. Peace has been preached to both. Then, using categories not derived from Israel, the author seizes another way of expressing his point—and it may have been a way that Gentiles could have understood quite well at that time: Christ creates in himself "one new humanity in place of the two" (2:15). The author's point is developed in the next verse: "and [Christ] might reconcile both groups to God *in one body*" (2:16): With that statement the image of "one new humanity" phases into the "body" image already noted. Whether it is the "one new humanity" or the "body of Christ," the author affirms the unity of Jews and Gentiles in the church.

In this section, we have seen that the author of Ephesians uses a wealth of interrelated images and metaphors to amplify his claims about the church and its place in God's plan. I now turn to other major features of the Letter to the Ephesians.

Admonitions for the Household

From Aristotle's time forward, there were codes of household duties, tables that suggested the proper attitudes and responsibilities for each of the groups that made up the households. Among other things, these tables or codes laid down the ways different people in the household should relate to the other members of it. From the culture around them, some early Christians took over the tables of instruction and guidance, the social codes of the times. To be sure, believers rarely co-opted any tradition or practice without adapting it to their new understanding of their situation in Christ and before God.

The later literature of the NT incorporates several of these household codes, but the lengthiest of them is in Ephesians (5:21—6:9; cf. Col. 3:18—4:1; 1 Pet. 2:18—3:7; 1 Tim. 2:8-12; 6:1-2; Titus 2:1-10). The author of Ephesians addresses each group of individuals in the households separately and directly: wives (5:22-24), husbands (5:25-33), children (6:1-3), fathers (6:4), slaves (6:5-8d), and masters (6:9). Whereas the material in chapter 4 and the early part of chapter 5 had instructed the faithful how they were to live with one another in the church, the material in the household code (5:21—6:9) instructs them how they ought to relate in the family setting. Their daily lives together are to reflect their new life in Christ. One does not live one way in the church and another in the household. In many respects the household is the microcosm of God's larger purposes, though the social unit is smaller and more intimate.

Ephesians' adoption of the household code, with its ranking of some groups as subordinate, shows that even though believers are to avoid the children of disobedience (2:2), the believers' structuring of their household relations probably looked much like that of the households of contemporary unbelievers.

The Eschatology of Ephesians

In the narrowest sense, eschatology is the study *(logos)* of the last things or end times *(eschaton)*. According to this restricted view, a judgment or final reckoning is expected at the end of history. A verdict will be passed on an individual's life, and the destiny of that person will depend on the way the verdict comes out. We know from the unquestioned Pauline letters, for example, that Paul anticipated he and all others would be judged at the end times (Rom. 14:10; 2 Cor. 5:10). The idea is widespread in early Christianity (cf. Matt. 25:31-46).

Although Ephesians lacks this explicit picture of God assessing and passing verdicts on persons' lives, it affirms the general idea, but with two differences. First, the immediacy of judgment is missing. Second, as we have seen, the judicial metaphors give way to other images preferred by the author. The "holy and blameless" requirements (1:4) do traditionally belong to the judgment scene, but Ephesians has transposed them into the context of the church's being presented as Christ's betrothed. Courtroom gives way to bridal chamber. The relation between judged and judge is formal, dreadful, and distant; that between bride and groom is infinitely more intimate and secure. In a letter so concerned to reassure and encourage, the marriage metaphor preserves a sense of future judgment but domesticates it.

Toward the letter's end, the author makes much the same point by shifting the image from marriage to warfare (6:10-17). Whereas with the marriage imagery the question is purity, in the battle context the issue is survival: "and having done everything, to stand firm" (6:13). To be found standing when the cosmic battle ends is to survive the final judgment.

Whether it is holiness or the capacity to be found standing, believers do not earn their status. It is gracefully given them. The faithful are enabled to stand because they are given God's armament *(panoplia)* through prayer (6:18); they are made holy because they are set apart for God in Christ.

In the course of downplaying the judicial picture of judgment at the end of history, the author of Ephesians has adopted a broader sense of eschatology. He shows no great interest in the last things, and certainly not in their immediacy. He asks instead: How does the future inform the lives the believers should live in the present? The believers must live in the knowledge that they will someday be presented as the bride before Christ. They live with an eye to the future in hopes of retaining the purity and blemishlessness given to them in the past and retained in the present. They prepare prayerfully for the battle by asking God's strength in the present. Insofar as the future is important in Ephesians, it serves to emphasize the present.

What I have thus far discussed about Ephesians' eschatology has been in temporal categories of past, present, and future. But in Ephesians the categories of time are supplemented by notions of space. Consider, for example, the fitting end of the first half of the letter (3:14-21). God's power is being celebrated. The author prays that the readers "may have the power to comprehend, with all the saints, what is the breadth and length and height and depth, and to know the love of Christ that surpasses knowledge"

(3:18-19). Categories of power and space blend into one another as the author attempts to describe what finally defies full description. It is as if the words of Ephesians signal an overload on the communications that need to be borne. The result: conceptions overlap; metaphors mix; thoughts pile up. Temporal expressions—as in past, present, and future—do not suffice to indicate the enormity of God's grace at work in God's plan. Spatial categories take center stage.

The peculiar spatial interest of Ephesians is nowhere better seen than in the central christological claim of chapter 1 and its development in chapter 2. Drawing on Psalm 110 and Psalm 8, the author of Ephesians fashions his fundamental affirmation concerning Christ: God "raised him from the dead and seated him at his right hand in the heavenly places" (1:20). Resurrection and ascension are fused. As a consequence of God's exalting Christ, Christ is "far above all rule and authority and power and dominion" (1:21). The same point is expressed differently in the next words: God "has put all things under his feet and has made him the head over all things" (1:22). Christ's exaltation and lordship are expressed in spatial categories.

The opening of chapter 2 applies those christological assertions to the readers: The God who raised Christ "from the dead and made him sit at his right hand in the heavenly places" (1:20) has "made us alive together with Christ . . . and raised us up with him and seated us with him in the heavenly places in Christ Jesus" (2:5-6). Christ was raised; the believers are raised with him. Christ was made to sit at God's right hand; the believers sit with him. The believers' solidarity with Christ is expressed by reusing the same verbs in both places. In chapter 2, the actions of the verbs are completed in the past. As a result, the present status of the believers is that they currently sit with Christ—already at the right hand of God in the heavenly places. The fact that the undisputed letters never make such a claim about resurrection already being a reality for believers shows how strongly the author of Ephesians has embraced spatial categories (see above on authorship).

Elsewhere in the letter, spatial categories are used to express the readers' previous alienation and their new, secure situation in Christ. Such a notion is in "separated from Christ" (*chōris Christou*, 2:12, RSV) and is high-lighted in the "far off" and "near" terminology of 2:13 (cf. also 2:17). Although the categories suggest a different sociological situation, "strang-ers" and "sojourners" suggest persons who are exiled from their home country, separated from their own place.

The author's point is basically the same whether he employs temporal claims, such as God "chose us in Christ before the foundation of the world" (1:4), or spatial ones, such as "you who once were far off have been brought near by the blood of Christ" (2:13). His rich use of spatial categories supplements and sometimes slightly modifies the more traditionally temporal assertions about what has been accomplished in Christ.

The Movement and Design of Ephesians

Interpreters of Ephesians have readily noted the way in which the conclusion of chapter 3, moving as it does toward the lofty praise of God's power and climaxing with the ascription to God (3:21-22), divides the letter into two parts. The second half of the document (chaps. 4–6) concerns itself with the entreaty and instruction so typical of the concluding sections of Paul's letters (cf. Romans 12 and 1 Thessalonians 4). But the instruction of the faithful is not confined to the second half of Ephesians; it is already interwoven in chapters 1–3. To be sure, the emphasis does shift after chapter 3: there is more instruction afterward than before. But there is a much more fundamental and revealing movement in the Letter to the Ephesians.

The Cosmic Scope of God's Plan.   After the salutation (cf. Rom. 1:1-7), Ephesians opens with the broadest possible vista. The author moves from before the creation of the world (1:4) to the consummation of God's plan for the fullness of time (1:10). Temporally, his vision reaches before history in the past and to its culmination in the future. Spatially, the scope is equally grand, moving from the world (1:4) through the heavenly places (1:3), including "things in heaven and things on earth" (1:10). Such is the cosmic, universal scope in which the author introduces his understanding of God's plan.

God's plan for the fullness of time is to "head up" *(anakephalaiōsasthai)* "all things" in Christ (1:10). The "all things" that are to be headed up together in cosmic unity in Christ and under his power include "things in heaven and things on earth" (1:10)—a broad vista indeed! The universe or cosmos is the arena where God's purposes are being realized.

Throughout the opening section (chaps. 1 and 2), the faithful are instructed concerning their place in God's eternal purpose (1:18). The readers are now alive in Christ and are included in God's plan through Christ's exaltation above all rival powers. By sharing Christ's exaltation (2:5-6) believers take their proper place in God's unfolding plan for the universe.

Thus the opening chapters of Ephesians set God's purposes in Christ against the backdrop provided by all of history and the universe itself. The place of the readers in history and in the universe is defined by their being "in Christ."

The first picture shown by the author of Ephesians is taken with a wide-angle lens. Nothing escapes the picture. Everything is included. The scope is vast. With chapter 3, however, it is as if the author has changed lenses and chooses to limit his scope a bit. What he gives up in breadth of view he gains in detail. Out of that vast first picture, the author chooses to focus on the believers and their role in God's plan. With that focus I move to the second picture.

Believers and Their Place in God's Purpose. In this second, more confined view, the believers are not passive bystanders or mere observers in the cosmic drama. They are the church, and as the church they have a special role to play. The church is given the task of revealing God's plan (3:10) to the powers that futilely contend with God for the allegiance of God's own creatures (cf. 2:2). Against the background provided by God's cosmic purpose, the church's role as revelatory agent is portrayed. It is noteworthy that the church's role is not confined to the earth, but like God's plan of which it is so important a part, the church plays a role not only in the earth but also in the heavens, where the "principalities and powers" may also be found (3:10).

Much of the material in the remainder of chapter 3, all of chapter 4, and some of chapter 5 has the church as its focus and describes how the faithful are to comport themselves with one another and in the world. They are to live in unity and in holiness appropriate to their baptism (cf. 4:1-6, 22-24).

After capturing the picture of the church in such detail, the author changes perspectives once more. From a focus on the cosmic church and its interrelationships, the author, in an ever-narrowing field of view, turns his attention to the next smallest social group of relevance for his readers, the household, and presents his third picture.

The Household of God. The lives of the faithful within the household are just as surely marked by God's plan. Their lives in the family must be attuned to God's larger purposes; there is no dichotomy between life in the community of believers and conduct within the family. For example, the spouses are to relate to one another as Christ and the church relate. They reflect God's cosmic plan being realized in the universe through Christ and the church. Likewise the other relationships in the household must correspond to what is known about God and God's purposes. For example, masters must relate to household slaves, knowing "that both of you have the same Master in heaven, and with him there is no partiality" (6:9).

Individuals as Part of God's Plan. Finally, in 6:10-20, the author makes his ultimate restriction of the scope and offers his fourth picture. This one addresses all individual believers equally, without respect to whether they may hold subordinate or dominant positions in the household. As God's cosmic purpose unfolds, all the faithful are to take upon themselves God's armament. It is God's battle that is to be won. The faithful are active participants, but, as surely as Roman soldiers did not equip themselves, believers do not provide their own armament. Ephesians is consistent: the power belongs to God. How do believers access God's power, here represented symbolically in terms of armament? The answer: "Pray in the Spirit at all times in every prayer and supplication" (6:18). When the faithful prayerfully take on the "whole armor of God" (6:11), they will "be strong in the Lord and in the strength of his power" (6:10). They will "be able to stand against the wiles of the devil" (6:11). Availing themselves of God's power, the faithful will be found standing when the victory is accomplished. Those standing after the battle will be the heirs of God's riches that God alone makes available in "the fullness of time" (1:10).

The overall design or movement of Ephesians, therefore, begins with the cosmic depiction of God's plan, God's purpose. Against the background provided by that depiction, the author describes the church and its role. Within the church the author sees the household as the next subunit. Finally, he addresses the individuals concerning their responsibilities as they attune themselves to God's larger purposes. The movement of Ephesians is as follows:

| God's cosmic plan | the church | the household | individuals |

As the focus narrows step-by-step, the author does not discard any of the context provided by the previous stage or stages. Indeed, the author confirms the continuity of the faithful life in the total context of God's plan even though his portrayal of it narrows as the letter progresses. No matter how narrow or wide the lens, the picture displays God's purposes at work and describes faithful participation.

One final detail is noteworthy. The author of Ephesians never resorts to stark or independent individualism. The community context of the life of faith is constantly in view. Even when describing the role of individuals (6:10-20), the "you" addressed is always the plural, never the singular. Furthermore, the prayer by which one dons the armor of God is not a self-serving prayer. It is a prayer "for all the saints" (6:18) and for the author (6:19). Even the prayer for the author is not directed to his personal welfare but toward his bold proclamation of the gospel (6:19-20). That closing note ties the entire address to the individuals back into the living and proclaiming of the gospel that is in large measure the revealing of God's cosmic plan. So the final admonition to individuals (6:10-20) leads directly back to the opening concern with proclaiming God's great and cosmic purposes for the faithful.

The Purpose of Ephesians—Revisited

When the letter explicitly calls the recipients "Gentiles" (2:11; 3:1, 6), the author is identified as a Jew because "Gentiles" was a Jewish catchall term for "everybody else." To call the recipients Gentiles is little more than to identify them as non-Jews. Those whom Jews labeled as Gentiles would have had means of self-identification other than "Gentile." Ephesians is a letter to former outsiders who are now viewed as insiders. Indeed, these new insiders are presumed so solidly reidentified as to allow the author to address them as *different from Gentiles:* "Now this I affirm and insist on in the Lord: you must no longer live as the Gentiles live" (4:17). This point is a major clue regarding the purpose of Ephesians. Ephesians is addressed to a readership who have experienced a radical transformation in their self-understanding, and the author not only recognizes that change in identity but also works diligently to confirm and enhance it.

In 2:11-13 the author establishes that the readers' outsider status as Gentiles was not so much an issue of their being non-Jews (v. 11). More fundamental was their being "separated from Christ" (v. 12, RSV). That separation has now been overcome. Because they are "now in Christ Jesus," they who were far off have been brought near (v. 13) and are no longer "aliens" and "strangers" to the "commonwealth of Israel" and the "covenants of promise" (v. 12). The readers' solidarity with Christ has removed their separation from the children of God, from Israel and from the covenants, and has replaced their outsider status with a strong new identification. Incorporation into God's household has come about through Christ.

The overriding purpose of Ephesians is identity formation. For this author, life is framed from baptism, the point of origin for this new identity, to the ultimate presentation of the believers as the bride of Christ. By transposing the well-known social patterns of the day—households, citizenships, marriages, battles, and the like—the author offers the readers a set of mutually reinforcing images through which they may be instructed, reassured, and rehearsed concerning who they are and how to live this new life together. In a world not destined for the imminent destruction that some other early church voices might have suggested, questions arise regarding how one lives not only with other believers but also in the ongoing world. Ephesians offers a cohesive, coherent view of life that details and affirms Christian identity and that gives rich guidelines for comportment.

COLOSSIANS

The Letter to the Colossians occupies a distinct and important place in the history of Christianity. In terms of its historical setting and impact, the letter sets forth teachings concerning Christ, his saving work, and his church that have had major and formative influences on the shaping of Christian doctrine. Moreover, the letter is of interest for showing how the struggle for these teachings was carried on in the first century against alternatives regarded as heretical. In modern times Colossians has been a major force and resource for theological reflection and proclamation, particularly in regard to such issues as the relationship between faith in Christ and ecological responsibility, the scope of Christ's redemptive work, and the future of the entire universe, including humanity.

The discussion to follow is divided into three major sections. The first takes up the place of Colossians within early Christianity, including such questions as authorship, purpose, and intended readers. The second deals with some of the major theological and ethical emphases of the letter. The third consists of an exegetical survey. From time to time commentaries and monographs on Colossians are mentioned, with full bibliographical information provided in the selected bibliography.

The Setting of Colossians
in Early Christianity

The Ancient Evidence

Ancient sources attribute the Letter to the Colossians to the apostle Paul. The letter itself asserts Pauline authorship three times (1:1, 23; 4:18), and it has the appearance of being a letter of Paul. Further, ancient references to the letter routinely assume Pauline authorship for it, including writers from the second century—both at the middle of that century (Marcion) and at its end (the Muratorian Canon; Irenaeus *Against Heresies* 3.14.1; Tertullian *Prescription Against Heresies* 7; and Clement of Alexandria *Stromateis* 1.1.17). Notations at the end of a few manuscripts (the so-called subscriptions) from the fifth century and later claim that the letter was written to Colossae "from Rome." But the prologue attached to some

Vulgate manuscripts of Colossians (one of the so-called Marcionite Prologues) claims that the letter was written "from Ephesus." Along with references within the letter to his imprisonment (4:3, 10, 18; cf. 1:24), the traditional picture that emerges is that Paul wrote the letter to the church at Colossae while he was imprisoned either in Rome or in Ephesus, and that it was carried to its destination by Tychicus and Onesimus (4:7-9).

Colossae, of which only ruins remain in modern times, was located in Phrygia (southwestern Asia Minor) in the valley of the Lycus River, which is one of the branches of the Meander. It was about one hundred miles east (and slightly south) of Ephesus, the chief city of the province of Asia, and a highway ran from Ephesus through Colossae and on to the east. The fifth- and fourth-century B.C. writings of Herodotus (*History* 7.30.1) and Xenophon (*Anabasis* 1.2.6) refer to Colossae as "large" and "prosperous and large," respectively, and by Paul's time it had been thoroughly hellenized. Nearby were the cities of Hierapolis (mentioned in Col. 4:13), about thirteen miles to the north, and Laodicea (mentioned in 2:1; 4:13, 15-16), about twelve miles northwest. According to Josephus (*Antiquities* 12.149), a number of Jewish families were forcibly settled in Phrygia in the early part of the second century B.C.; nevertheless, the great majority of the population would have been Gentiles. The belief is widespread that the city was destroyed by an earthquake in A.D. 60 or 61, although the evidence is not decisive. According to Tacitus (*Annals* 14.27), such an earthquake destroyed nearby Laodicea—but he says that that city was rebuilt soon (which references to it in Rev. 1:11; 3:14 confirm)—and Colossae may well have been destroyed along with it, as Eusebius (fourth century) and Orosius (fifth century) claimed. There are no known references to Colossae or to the Christian community there for the rest of the first century. The conclusion to be drawn is that the city had probably been leveled when Laodicea was. Not until the middle of the second century can one find references to it again, and the site seems to have been abandoned as a place of habitation for good in the eighth century.

From the letter itself it appears that the church at Colossae had been founded not by Paul but by Epaphras, a coworker of Paul (1:7) and a native of Colossae (4:12). Neither Colossians, Acts, nor any other ancient source claims that Paul had ever been at Colossae. According to Colossians, however, the imprisoned apostle became aware that the Christian community at Colossae had become a mission field for false teachers who taught a "philosophy" (2:8) that called for ascetic and ritualistic practices (2:16-23), which Christians must reject. The purpose of the letter then was to combat the so-called Colossian heresy and to exhort the community to maintain the freedom that is theirs in Christ and the life that flows from mature faith (1:28; 4:12).

Contemporary Assessments about Authorship

The picture created so far seems plausible, and a good number of current scholars find it satisfactory. Nevertheless, beginning with a commentary on Colossians by E. T. Mayerhoff (1838), questions have been raised about the authorship of the letter and its place in early Christianity. The view of many today is that the letter is pseudonymous, the product of a Pauline loyalist of the "Pauline school." The considerations that lead to that assessment are quite compelling, and some of them are reviewed here.

First, the Letter to the Colossians contains terms and expressions that are not found in the seven undisputed letters of Paul (Romans, 1 and 2 Corinthians, Galatians, Philippians, 1 Thessalonians, and Philemon). These are illustrated in detail in the work of Walter Bujard and in less detail in major commentaries, such as those by Eduard Lohse and Petr Pokorný. Lohse (84–91) provides a list of thirty-four words appearing in Colossians that are hapax legomena (words that occur only once in the NT), such as *philosophia* (philosophy), *theotēs* (deity), *eirēnopoiein* (to make peace), and *eucharistos* (thankful); and fifty-three words that appear in Colossians and elsewhere in the NT, but not in the seven undisputed letters of Paul, such as *syndoulos* (fellow servant), *aphesis* (forgiveness), and *dogma* (regulation). Conversely, some important Pauline words do not appear in Colossians, such as *hamartia* (sin), *dikaiosynē* (justification), *dikaioun* (to justify), *sōtēria* (salvation), *nomos* (law), *eleutheria* (freedom), and *hypakoē* (obedience). On the one hand, in terms of style, the writer of Colossians tends to use longer sentences than those typically found in Paul's undisputed letters; he is fond of heaping up series of dependent genitives (literally, e.g., 1:5, "the word of truth of the gospel"; 1:13, "the kingdom of the son of his love"; 1:27, "the riches of the glory of this mystery," etc.); and he frequently places synonyms together (e.g., 1:9, "praying . . . and asking"; 1:22, "holy and blameless and irreproachable"; and 1:26, "the ages and generations"). On the other hand, writes Pokorný, "The indicators of Paul's rhetorical directness . . . are not to be found in Colossians" (2).

In addition to matters of vocabulary and style, Colossians contains theological expressions and concepts that differ from those found in the undisputed Paulines. Lacking are any discussions of law, justification, sin, and the role of the Spirit in relation to baptism (2:12), the new life (3:9-17), and "in checking the indulgence of the flesh" (2:23, my trans.). It is often said that justification is not an important theme in Paul's letters outside Romans and Galatians, and that its absence in Colossians does not therefore speak against Pauline authorship. But it seems that one is entitled to expect it if Paul had been the author of Colossians, for it could have been used as a weapon in combat with the opponents at Colossae, who promoted "regulations" (2:20) for attaining wisdom.

Colossians does, of course, set forth a "Pauline" theology, as do other letters that are suspected of being deutero-Pauline. Familiar Pauline themes are found, but they have been extended or modified in new directions. Christ is portrayed as mediator of creation (1:16), triumphant over the principalities and powers (2:10, 15), and the one in whom "the whole fullness of deity dwells bodily" (2:9). Moreover, Christ is "head of the body, the church" (1:18). Although the "cosmic Christology" thus presented and its attendant ecclesiology have roots in the undisputed letters of Paul (see below), they mark transitions that fit better into a post-Pauline situation. That is true also in regard to eschatology, in which the concept of an imminent return of Christ is lacking, and in the twin concepts of faith, which in Colossians is *fides quae creditur* (faith that is believed in; cf. 1:23; 2:7), and hope, which is now not so much an expectant attitude of the believer (the usual Pauline sense of hope) as something hoped for, an object that is "laid up . . . in heaven" (1:5; cf. 1:23, 27).

The evidence cited here—matters of language and style and nuances of theological content—is evaluated differently by various scholars in drawing conclusions about authorship. In general there are three major views, which can be illustrated from the commentaries listed in the bibliography. First, F. F. Bruce (28–33) and Peter O'Brien (xli–liv) conclude that, in spite of the acknowledged differences, one can still consider the letter to have been written by Paul. Along with them can be listed Ralph Martin (98–99), who says that his "persuasion is to stay with Paul's authorial responsibility for the letter, though with some hesitation." Second, Eduard Schweizer (15–26) suggests that, although the letter was neither written nor dictated by Paul and must be considered pseudonymous, an associate of Paul (perhaps Timothy) could have written it during the lifetime of Paul, perhaps during an imprisonment of Paul at Ephesus. Third, Eduard Lohse (180–83) and Petr Pokorný (3–21) consider the letter to be pseudonymous and written in the post-Pauline situation. When the evidence is taken cumulatively, the conclusion that the letter is pseudonymous appears most compelling, and I take that view in this essay.

One of the objections to that point of view is that, if Colossae was destroyed in A.D. 60–61, why would a letter be written to a community there after the death of Paul (ca. A.D. 62)? Presumably no community would have existed! The response of Pokorný (20–21) to that question is well considered. The destruction of Colossae in the early 60s would have been a perfect setup for a pseudonymous letter. No one would have been able to deny that the community had received such a letter from Paul. Further, the letter was to be read "also in the church of the Laodiceans"

(4:16) a few miles away, a community that was rebuilt shortly after the earthquake had destroyed it. Other indications within the letter also suggest that Laodicea was an actual destination for it (2:1; 4:15)—and probably Hierapolis too (4:13). The "Colossian heresy" would then have flourished in the region after the destruction of Colossae itself, particularly at Laodicea and Hierapolis. Thus someone of the Pauline school wrote this letter to refute those who promoted the heresy and delivered the letter, or had it delivered, in the communities of Asia Minor that were being threatened. Who that person was (Timothy, Tychicus, Epaphras, or whoever) remains unknown. As for time and place of composition, the decade of the 60s after the death of Paul, or perhaps even the 70s (but before the writing of Ephesians, which is dependent on Colossians), and in à Pauline school at Ephesus are the most likely possibilities.

The "Colossian Heresy"

The so-called Colossian heresy has been mentioned a few times in passing, and some discussion of it is necessary before leaving the question of the setting of Colossians in early Christianity. From the letter itself, our only source, a composite can be drawn, even though a label is difficult to attach to it. It is called a "philosophy" (2:8), but what kind is it? The author describes it only indirectly by speaking of his opponents (2:8-23). Apparently they promote a syncretistic worldview (cosmology) accompanied by asceticism, moral rigorism, and ritual obligations. For them, the "elemental spirits of the universe" (2:8, 20), conceived as angelic and heavenly powers (2:10, 15, 18), govern human and cosmic destinies. Such a viewpoint is expressed in both Gentile Hellenistic and Jewish Hellenistic texts prior to the rise of Christianity. Those texts use various names to designate the cosmic powers—thrones, dominions, principalities, authorities, powers (cf. 1:16; 2:15), and elements of the universe. In pagan Hellenism they are sometimes identified with the heavenly bodies (planets and stars) and are regarded as gods. In Hellenistic Judaism they cannot be, and are not, regarded as gods, for the heavenly bodies have been created by God, who has set them in their courses (Pss. 8:3; 136:9; Jer. 31:35). Yet on the basis of Gen. 1:16 (cf. Ps. 136:9), which states that the sun and moon "rule" by day and night, it was possible for some Jews to regard "the sun, the moon, the stars, and all the created objects which circulate in all the chariots of heaven" as having a ruling function "in the face of the sky and be seen on the earth" (*1 Enoch* 75:3). In the Hellenistic Jewish *Testament of Solomon*, as in Colossians, the "elements" (*stoicheia*) are identified with heavenly bodies; they have a ruling function and are malevolently disposed to the human race (8:1-4; 18:1-3).

The advocates of the philosophy being proposed promote the worship (or veneration) of angels (Col. 2:18a), which they may have thought to be the actual powers that move the heavenly bodies (the "elements") and which must be placated. The meaning of the phrase "worship of angels" in 2:18, however, is a matter of dispute. Fred Francis (*Conflict at Colossae*, 176–81) has interpreted the phrase to mean "the worship which the angels perform"—a worship in which the heretical teachers themselves claimed to participate, and in which they encouraged the Colossians to join, by means of a mystical ascent. The thesis is attractive and has been adopted in the commentary by Peter O'Brien (142–43). Yet other interpreters have rejected it for the following reasons: (1) there is evidence that some ancient Phrygian cults included the (human) worship (or veneration) of angels; and (2) at 2:23 the writer speaks negatively about *ethelothrēskia* (worship practices taken on voluntarily), the worship that people themselves do, which refers back to the worship (*thrēskeia*) prescribed by the heretical teachers at 2:18. The traditional view is that the "worship of angels" would have consisted of cultic acts conducted to gain the favor of angels, the would-be rulers of the universe.

Beyond these matters, the heretical teachers advocate mysticism (2:18b)—not necessarily related to the "worship of angels" but in addition to that—and adherence to selected aspects of Jewish law, including circumcision (2:11), dietary regulations (2:16a), Sabbath and festival observances (2:16b), and laws of purity (2:20-21). All these regulations have "an appearance of wisdom" in promoting discipline (2:23). The implication seems to be that through such a way of wisdom one can master the secrets of the universe so that upon death one's purified and disciplined soul can ascend through the spheres of the "elements" and "angels" and return to its heavenly home.

Interpreters have sought to identify the religious and philosophical backgrounds to the Colossian heresy, but precision seems elusive. With few exceptions, scholars in the twentieth century have concluded that the heresy at Colossae had a basis in some form of Judaism, plus elements from other sources. Lohse (127–31) and Pokorný (113–20) suggest that the other elements came from "pre-Gnostic teaching" or an early form of Gnosticism, respectively. Schweizer (125–33) advances Jewish Pythagoreanism as a basis for the heresy. Bruce (17–26) thinks that Jewish mysticism (related to Jewish Gnosticism) will suffice. Fred Francis and Thomas Sappington contend that the roots of the heresy can be traced to an ascetic-mystical piety in Hellenistic Judaism. Martin (90–96) proposes that the heresy consisted of a dualistic syncretism based on Jewish traditions and speculative ideas from Greek religion. O'Brien (xxx–xxxviii) proffers a Jewish Christian ascetic background plus pagan elements from Phrygia. Günther

Bornkamm has suggested the most elaborate background: a combination of elements from "gnosticized Judaism," Persian religion, Chaldean astronomy, and Christianity.

As one can see, labels do not fit easily in describing the heresy and its background. The heretics obviously made much of the Jewish heritage (whether they themselves were Jewish or not) but had an aggressive mission to Gentiles—not necessarily to pagan Gentiles but certainly to Gentiles who were Christians already. In that regard, their movement was parasitical, and the author of Colossians sought to expel their influence. How successful he was cannot be known. That the letter was preserved—and even became a source for the writing of Ephesians—indicates that the writer must have had at least a hearing and some success in his efforts.

Major Theological and Ethical Emphases

Christology and Soteriology

Christology is the author's main weapon in confronting the heretical teachers. He uses the usual christological titles found in the letters of Paul— Christ, Lord, and son of God. Moreover, he affirms Christ's crucifixion (1:20); his resurrection (2:12); his reign in heaven, where he is seated at God's right hand (3:1); and his coming again in the future (3:4). All these points are familiar from the Pauline tradition. In addition, the author speaks of Christ as "head of the body, the church" (1:18) and "head of every ruler and authority" (2:10).

The "cosmic" significance of Christ is one of the most distinctive aspects of Colossians. Most of the material that sets forth this aspect of Christology is contained in 1:15-20, which can be regarded as a hymn concerning him. But not all of it is found there (cf. 2:3, 10, 15; 3:1), so it cannot be considered alien to the thought of the writer. Christ is "the firstborn of all creation" (1:15). Although that formualtion might sound like Arianism (that Christ was a created being), it is more likely that it signifies his status as superior to *all* creation. Further, Christ has a role in the creation of the universe. Drawing on the wisdom tradition in Israel (Prov. 8:22-31; Wisd. of Sol. 9:1-4), the writer applies the role of Wisdom as God's agent in the creation of the universe to Christ. He is therefore superior to all the cosmic powers that the false teachers speak of in their mission. Finally, in one of the clearest expressions of a "high Christology" in the NT, the writer speaks of Christ as the one in whom "the whole fullness of deity [*theotēs*] dwells bodily" (2:9). That is, Christ is the one who reveals God most fully; he is the one in whom God is encountered as the gospel is proclaimed and heard. One does not encounter God by means of the visions of mystical experience, contrary to the teaching of the opponents (2:18).

Colossians lacks the Pauline concept of sin as a power reigning over humanity. Instead the writer speaks of "sins" (plural), "evil deeds," and "trespasses" (1:14, 21; 2:13) for which there must be forgiveness, and forgiveness has been accomplished by Christ's sacrificial death on the cross (1:22; 2:13-14). Nevertheless, according to the opponents, there are the powers that rule over humanity, the cosmic powers referred to in the author's polemics and debates. But according to the author of the letter, those powers are no real threat to persons who are "in Christ." Christ has "disarmed" the powers, rendering them impotent, by his triumph over them (2:15). Since those in Christ are reconciled to God, they have nothing to fear. Peace has been established between God and his people (1:20).

Ecclesiology

The term "church" shows up in the letter to designate the church as extended ("universal") fellowship (1:18, 24) and as a local community—both as a "house church" (4:15) and as the community of believers in a given city (4:16). In matters of church order, the letter is all but silent. Paul is an apostle (1:1) and minister (*diakonos*, 1:23, 25) of the gospel. The term "minister" is also applied to Epaphras at 1:7 and to Tychicus at 4:7, but it seems to be a general designation for one who serves the gospel of Christ rather than an office that is attached to work in any given community. Other than the office of apostle, which Paul alone is known to have, it appears that the community knows no fixed offices at all. Preaching and instruction occur as members of the community "admonish one another in all wisdom" (3:16).

The ecclesiology of the letter is bound up closely with its Christology: Christ is "head of the body, the church" (1:18; cf. 2:19). Paul had already used the metaphor of "the body of Christ" for the church (Rom. 12:5; 1 Cor. 12:27). But the author of Colossians goes a step further than Paul with his concept of the head-body/Christ-church relationship. It allows him to envision Christ as ruling over the world from heaven ("above," 3:1) through his church on earth, the visible, earthly manifestation of "the kingdom of [God's] beloved Son" (1:13). Its members are a "holy" and "chosen" people (1:22; 3:12) who belong to "one body" (3:15) and "set [their] minds on things that are above" (3:2). In their worship the word of God is proclaimed, and the congregation sings "psalms, hymns, and spiritual songs" (3:16). Members of the church are expected to be unpretentious in deportment, forgiving, and loving (3:12-14).

Moral Teaching

As in the case of Paul's undisputed letters (cf. 1 Cor. 13:13), love is emphasized above all in the moral teaching of Colossians: love is that which "binds everything together in perfect harmony" (Col. 3:14). In addition, the writer lists a number of virtues—compassion, kindness, lowliness, meekness, and patience (3:12)—that are also familiar from the genuine letters of Paul.

The foundation on which the moral teaching of the letter rests is baptism into the death and resurrection of Christ, which is a means of death to the old life and being "made alive" with Christ by divine power (2:12-13). In consequence of baptism, the believer has "received" Christ and is "rooted and built up in him" (2:6-7). What follows is the rejection of worldly values (2:20; 3:2) and the life that they produce (3:5), and at the same time the taking on of a new life, a new nature (3:10), that grows toward maturity (1:28; 4:12).

One of the more obvious features of the moral teaching of Colossians is the presence of the "household codes" (German *Haustafeln*) in 3:18— 4:1, listing the duties of wives, husbands, children, fathers, slaves, and masters. Such codes are found in other Deutero-Paulines (cf. Eph. 5:22— 6:9; 1 Tim. 2:8-15; 6:1-2; Titus 2:1-10), but not in the genuine Pauline letters themselves. In his analysis of such codes, James Crouch has concluded that the purpose of the household codes in Colossians was to oppose the teachings of the heretical teachers. According to him, the latter represented a form of "enthusiasm" that abolished distinctions in society (not simply within gatherings for worship), particularly those between slaves and masters and between the sexes. The writer of Colossians reflects a socially conservative ethic, insisting that Christians conduct themselves "wisely toward outsiders, making the most of the time" (4:5). He writes for a community that must, in his view, come to terms with living in the world for an indeterminate time.

Reading the Letter: An Exegetical Survey

The structure of Colossians corresponds to that of the typical Pauline letter. After an opening (1:1-2) there is a thanksgiving section, in which the author gives thanks to God for the faith and love of the recipients and anticipates the message of the remainder of the letter (1:3-14). Then comes the body of the letter (1:15—4:6), which can be broken down generally into two main sections, a doctrinal one (1:15—2:23) and a hortatory one (3:1— 4:6). A conclusion follows that contains instructions, greetings, and a brief benediction (4:7-18). The survey here follows this major outline.

Opening, 1:1-2

The opening has the familiar form: names of senders (Paul and Timothy), names of recipients (persons at Colossae), and a greeting. The writer is (supposedly) Paul, who alone is designated as an apostle, and who associates Timothy with himself as sender of the letter (using words identical to those of 2 Cor. 1:1). The mention of Timothy does not mean that he was a coauthor of the letter (although some modern scholars have suggested that Timothy was the actual writer). He is Paul's coworker in preaching and teaching the gospel, and mention of his name may serve to show the readers of the letter that the message that follows has a base of support in the wider Christian fellowship. The writer speaks of the recipients as "saints and faithful brothers and sisters in Christ in Colossae." As in the genuine Pauline letters, the "in Christ" formula (cf. 1:28) is used to signify that those to whom it applies have been gathered into a fellowship under Christ's dominion. The opening ends with a brief greeting, which mentions only God the Father; usually Christ is mentioned in Pauline greetings as well. The declaration of "grace" and "peace" from God—always appearing in the Pauline letters—is extended to the recipients. While the usual Hellenistic letter opened with *chairein* (meaning "hail" or "greetings"), Paul uses and combines *charis* (grace) and *eirēnē* (peace; from the Hebrew greeting *shalom*), thereby alluding to the favor of God newly made manifest in Christ, and at the same time maintaining continuity with the traditional greeting among God's people.

Thanksgiving, 1:3-14

As in the genuine letters of Paul (except for Galatians), a thanksgiving section follows that expresses thanks to God and projects important themes in the letter. Here the writer gives thanks to God for the faith in Christ and the love for the saints that have characterized the community at Colossae. The writer knows of their faith and love because it has been reported to him by Epaphras (1:8-9), who apparently founded the Christian community there (1:7). Because of their faithful Christian witness, the author says that he makes continual thanksgiving and intercessions for them (1:3, 9).

The section contains some concepts and themes that will be developed further in the letter. The word "hope" (1:5) appears later (1:23, 27), but it has already been given its essential content here. It is "hope which is hoped for" (Lohse, 17), an objective goal that is laid up in heaven and that the believer in Christ expects to possess beyond this life. Above all, the passage anticipates the author's concern that the recipients increase in knowledge, wisdom, and understanding and that they live lives that are expected of believers. The author develops this theme later as he urges growth and maturity in faith (1:28; 2:6; 3:10; 4:12) and exhorts his readers several times to live lives that are consistent with their union with Christ through baptismal death and regeneration (cf. 2:12, 20; 3:1, 5, 12-17).

The section closes with an assertion that has the sound of creedal origins (1:13-14). God has rescued his people from one realm, that of darkness, and has set them in another, Christ's kingdom, where there is redemption, the forgiveness of sins. If the verses had a creedal or liturgical origin, they were most likely used in connection with baptism, which would have been celebrated as the moment in which the believer's transfer to the dominion of Christ takes place. In any case, through their belonging to Christ, believers have redemption, a present reality, the forgiveness of sins. As various interpreters have indicated, the writer of Colossians sees the work of Christ as having been accomplished, and there is an accent on salvation as a present reality for those who are in Christ (2:12-13; 3:1). Yet the future aspect of salvation in its fullness is still expected (cf. 3:4, 6, 24).

The Body: Doctrinal Section, 1:15—2:23

The body of the letter opens immediately with what almost all interpreters regard as a hymn incorporated by the writer into the letter (1:15-20). The hymn could well have been familiar to his readers. The author may have altered it somewhat, however, by adding words characteristic of his own purposes and theology: "the church" (1:18) and "through the blood of his cross" (1:20), as some commentators hold. In any case, in its present form the hymn has two stanzas or strophes. The first (1:15-18a) has to do with Christ and his role in creation; the second (1:18b-20) with his role in redemption. By calling Christ the "firstborn of all creation" (declaring his uniqueness) and the one in whom, through whom, and for whom all things were created, the hymn writer draws on the wisdom tradition of Israel. In Prov. 8:22-31 "Wisdom" is personified as God's agent in creating the cosmos. The same can be found in Hellenistic Jewish sources, particularly in the Wisdom of Solomon (9:1-4). Against the wisdom background of ancient Judaism, the hymn writer—like the apostle Paul (1 Cor. 8:6) and the authors of the Fourth Gospel (1:1-3) and Hebrews (1:1-3)—identifies Christ with the preexistent Wisdom who has created all things. The "all things" created include the cosmic powers that the opponents at Colossae proclaim as all-powerful forces ruling the world, including human lives. The cosmic powers cannot therefore be superior to Christ, for he was instrumental in bringing them about in the first place.

The second strophe (1:18b-20), celebrating Christ's role in redemption, affirms not only his resurrection but its temporal and ontological significance. Christ—and no one else—has been raised from death and given preeminence over all things. As the "firstborn from the dead," he heads up the new humanity, the church, and in fact is preeminent among all things ever created. Even in his earthly life he incarnated the "fullness of God" (1:19), which led to his reconciling work at the cross. The scope of Christ's reconciling work is universal—"all things, whether on earth or in heaven" (1:20). By means of his death and subsequent resurrection, Christ reigns over all things; everything in the universe is subject to him, and universal peace has been established. Christ's triumphal reign may not be evident, but it is known to faith, and that means within the context of this letter that "the way home to God" is not a dangerous and malevolent path that has to be maneuvered among the hostile powers, but is certain and safe because of Christ's triumph over them.

While the hymn speaks of the reconciliation of all things, the writer of Colossians wants above all to address the situation of his readers. At 1:21 therefore he switches from the cosmological level to the personal and existential dimensions of reconciliation, using the emphatic "and you" (plural) and at 1:22 the emphatic "now." The readers were at one time alienated and morally adrift. But now they have been "reconciled." Christ took upon himself the sins of humanity and bore in himself the penalty to its ultimate conclusion, death. As a consequence, those formerly estranged and under condemnation are blameless; their sins have been forgiven (cf. 1:14; 3:13), and they are "holy and blameless and irreproachable" (1:22).

From 1:24 through 2:7 the writer, impersonating Paul, speaks of the suffering and role of the apostle "to make the word of God fully known" (1:25). He says that by means of his suffering he completes "what is lacking in Christ's afflictions" (1:24)—a statement, it seems, that Paul would hardly make. Paul does on occasion speak of sharing in Christ's sufferings (2 Cor. 1:5) and being given up to death for Jesus' sake (2 Cor. 4:11). But in those instances he speaks of his suffering as the means by which he brings the gospel, and therefore life, to other people (2 Cor. 4:12). There is no hint in Paul's writings, and probably not here in Colossians, that the atoning sufferings of Christ were insufficient for redemption. The author probably means that in the time between Christ's resurrection and parousia those afflictions which belong to Christ and his people (the "messianic woes" of apocalyptic) are being completed for the sake of "his body, the church" in the apostle's particular mission.

This part of Colossians portrays Paul as the ideal apostle, presently imprisoned and concerned about readers in a community he has not visited (2:1, 5), who has a special role in revealing the content of the "mystery" of God that has been hidden from the beginning of time. The term "mystery" (*mystērion*) appears three times in this portion of the letter (1:26, 27; 2:2) and again toward the end (4:3). The term has a rich background in Jewish sources and signifies knowledge hidden from eternity, unknown to both angels and humanity in general but revealed to and made known by certain trusted persons chosen by God. Here the content of the mystery is the saving activity of God that has been revealed to Paul and through him "to his saints," and made known to the world in their proclamation of the gospel of Christ. Through such proclamation and teaching there is "wisdom" and "knowledge" (1:28; 2:3) that lead to true maturity. Although he cannot be present at Colossae or Laodicea, Paul carries on a struggle for them, that they may not be deceived but be encouraged, united in love (2:2-4), and established "in the faith" once taught by his trusted coworker Epaphras (2:7).

The rest of the doctrinal section (2:8-23) is actually hortatory, a warning against the false teachers. The content of their teaching (the "Colossian heresy") has been described above and need not be repeated here. The author contends that no concessions can be made to the false teachers: one must either follow them or the Pauline gospel; there is no middle way. Through baptism into Christ, the believer has been "buried," "raised," and "made alive" with Christ, the crucified and resurrected one. (The burial metaphor, used already by Paul at Rom. 6:4, is apt; as one does not bury oneself, so one does not baptize oneself; the community does both in consequence of death or conversion.) Baptism is also the all-sufficient act by which one becomes a person "in Christ," a "circumcision made without hands" (2:11, NRSV margin), and no supplements are needed (asceticism, the observance of days, or mystical experiences). Those who have been baptized have already "come to fullness" in Christ and have received forgiveness (2:10, 13); they belong to the one who is now triumphant over the powers that, according to the false teachers, must still be placated. All the heretical demands spelled out in 2:16-23—although they may have the "appearance of wisdom" (2:23)—are actually futile. To submit to them is to live "as if" one still belongs to the world (2:20). Instead the author exhorts his readers to "hold fast" to Christ, the "head," upon whom the body (the church) is totally and alone dependent. Under the guidance of Christ (the head), the church (his body) is bound together and experiences the "growth that is from God" (2:19).

The Body: Hortatory Section, 3:1—4:6

The antiheretical section (2:8-23) is largely hortatory already, calling on the readers to avoid the false teachers. But 3:1 marks the beginning of a series of exhortations on matters that go beyond that specific concern. The opening verses (3:1-4) indicate a transition. Using spatial imagery, the writer thinks in terms of two realms, the earthly and the heavenly. Christ is in the realm "above," and his kingdom is a present reality that extends from above down upon and includes the church (1:13); it is not simply a future hope. Since believers actually belong to the kingdom of Christ (indicative), they are to set their minds on "things that are above, not on things that are on earth" (3:2, the imperative that follows from the indicative). By saying that the believers' lives are "hidden with Christ in God," the writer holds in check any idea that the fullness of their final salvation is unambiguously evident in the present. That fullness will be apparent only at the parousia (3:3-4).

In 3:5-11 the writer lists those "earthly things" that are to be avoided. The vices are to be "put to death" (v. 5) and "put away" (v. 8, RSV). They are typical of vices listed elsewhere in the Pauline and Deutero-Pauline letters (cf. especially Gal. 5:19-21 and 2 Tim. 3:2-5). In general they are vices related to sexual misconduct, covetousness, idolatry, anger, and deceit. The writer makes a sharp distinction between the "old self [*palaios anthrōpos*]" and the "new self [*neos anthrōpos*]" (Col. 3:9-10); the former must be cast away, and the latter must be put on (as with clothing)—the new self is being renewed in knowledge in accord with the image of God. In the newness that comes from such a transformation, earthly distinctions among persons (Jew/Gentile and slave/free) pass away (3:11). The verse is reminiscent of Gal. 3:28, although the Pauline "neither male nor female" is conspicuously absent.

In Col. 3:12-17 the virtues that are to characterize the lives of "God's chosen ones [*eklektoi tou theou*]" (3:12) are set forth. The terms used are known already from the letters of Paul, but there they are qualities of God or Christ. Here they are the virtues that are to be "put on" as a garment; they are thus to characterize one's outer relationships with others. (As 3:5 has a series of five main vices, 3:12 has a series of five main virtues.) But the main thing to "put on" is love (*agapē*), by which one makes others objects of selfless concern and service, and "which binds everything together in perfect harmony" (3:14). From this point follows a series of exhortations concerning peace within the community, worship (necessarily incorporating the word of God and song), and giving thanks to God.

The hortatory section draws to a close with a series of "household codes" (3:18—4:1). Duties are spelled out for wives, husbands, children, fathers, slaves, and masters. As indicated above, such codes do not appear in the undisputed letters of Paul. The duties prescribed for persons in the various stations of life listed are rather conventional in actual practice, but again and again (in nearly every verse) they are given a distinct motivation: serving or pleasing the Lord. They reflect a conservative social ethic but one that is world affirming—contrary to the prescriptions of the heretical teachers. The brief exhortations that conclude the body of the letter (4:2-6) call attention to the apostle's imprisonment and make requests. Prayer is requested for Paul and his preaching of the word of God, so the request "that God will open to us a door for the word" (4:3) must obliquely include petition for Paul's release from prison. The final two verses highlight the social conservativism of the letter (4:5-6).

Conclusion, 4:7-18

A conclusion containing greetings and a benediction—and sometimes additional items—is found in all the letters of Paul (Galatians, however, lacks final greetings). The conclusion to Colossians is similar to those in Paul's letters, although it is more detailed than most. It begins with references to Tychicus and Onesimus, who are apparently the ones who are to carry the letter to its destination. They will, however, do more than deliver the letter; they will also bring oral information concerning the apostle (4:7, 9). Tychicus was a resident of Asia Minor (cf. Acts 20:4), and references to him both in this letter and in other Deutero-Paulines (Eph. 6:21; 2 Tim. 4:12; Titus 3:12) cause one to suspect that he may have been a major figure in the so-called Pauline school at Ephesus after the death of Paul. Onesimus and later Epaphras (4:9, 12) are identified as persons from the Colossian community. This Onesimus must be the same person mentioned in Paul's Letter to Philemon. Epaphras was the founder of the Christian community at Colossae (1:7), and he had been a fellow prisoner of Paul (Philem. 23).

Greetings are sent from three persons (Aristarchus, Mark, and Jesus Justus), who are explicitly designated as Jewish Christians, and then from three others (Epaphras, Luke, and Demas). All of these, minus Jesus Justus, send greetings at the end of the Letter to Philemon.

The community is instructed to transmit greetings to the community at Laodicea, as well as to the church at the house of Nympha (location unspecified), and to swap letters with the church of the Laodiceans. A first-century letter of Paul to the Laodiceans, to which the verse refers, does not exist; perhaps it did at one time. In any case, that the city of Colossae may well have been destroyed by the time that Colossians was written, and that Colossians is to be read at Laodicea could mean that the latter city was its true destination. More revealing in these verses is the evidence that the letters of Paul were being sent about from church to church by the time that Colossians was written, and that circulation made it possible for their being collected together in a Pauline corpus.

The letter concludes with a handwritten greeting from Paul (cf. Gal. 6:11; 1 Cor. 16:21; 2 Thess. 3:17), a reminder of his imprisonment, and an exceedingly brief benediction. Consisting of only four words (Greek text, but also in English translation), it is shorter than what is found in the undisputed letters of Paul, corresponding to the closing words of 1 Tim. 6:21: "Grace be with you." Thus the letter ends, as it began (1:2), with a declaration of grace (divine favor), which is the basis for the redemptive work of God in Christ—and for the continued existence of the church.

2 THESSALONIANS

A Letter from Paul?

Second Thessalonians was the first letter bearing Paul's name that prompted scholars to question its Pauline authorship. While some interpreters regarded 2 Thessalonians as a pseudonymous writing, others tried to safeguard Pauline authorship in a variety of ways. Hugo Grotius (1640) already argued that 2 Thessalonians was written *prior* to 1 Thessalonians. This hypothesis was taken up in the twentieth century (e.g., J. Weiss, T. W. Manson, J. C. Hurd in *IDBSup* [cf. Bibliography in R. Jewett, *The Thessalonian Correspondence*], and the recent commentary by Charles Wanamaker). But the reversal of the traditional order of 1 and 2 Thessalonians does not remove the problems connected with 2 Thess. 3:17 and 2:2. The reference to *"every* letter" bearing his authenticating sign (3:17) presupposes that other Pauline letters exist and are known to the addressees. Moreover, the appearance during Paul's lifetime of a forged letter to which 2:2 refers is rather improbable (the forgery would also constitute the earliest known reference to a letter from Paul). Finally, the problem of the incongruous eschatology between the two letters is not solved by a reversal of the traditional order. If one holds that 2 Thessalonians is an authentic letter written by Paul prior to 1 Thessalonians, then one is also forced to assume that Paul initially taught the Thessalonians—by word of mouth when he "was still with" them (2 Thess. 2:5) and subsequently by his first letter, our 2 Thessalonians—that the "coming [*parousia*] of our Lord Jesus Christ" (2:1) was quite distant in accordance with the apocalyptic timetable of 2:3-12. Then, a few weeks later, when writing 1 Thessalonians, he had changed his mind and now held that the parousia was imminent (cf. 1 Thess. 4:17). In short, a reversal of the order of these two letters does not commend itself.

Adolf von Harnack (cf. Bibliography in R. Jewett, *The Thessalonian Correspondence*) tried to show that 2 Thessalonians had been addressed to the Jewish Christian minority of Thessalonica, whereas 1 Thessalonians was to be read to the whole church. But the text of 2 Thessalonians gives no indication that it was meant for only a segment within the church. On the contrary, the address (1:1), the reference to "every one of you all" (1:3, AV), the inclusive "all" in 3:16, 18, and Paul's general advocacy of unity within the community of believers make Harnack's thesis untenable. Recognizing this difficulty, Martin Dibelius suggested that 1 Thessalonians was directed to the leaders of the church, while 2 Thessalonians was addressed to the whole community. But 1 Thess. 5:27, which requests that "this letter be read to all the brothers" and sisters (cf. NRSV margin), would seem to contradict this hypothesis. One might also ask why the admonition to respect the leaders of the community (1 Thess. 5:12) should be addressed to the leaders rather than to the members of the church.

The most comprehensive recent defense of the authenticity of 2 Thessalonians is found in Robert Jewett's *The Thessalonian Correspondence,* and in the commentary by Charles Wanamaker. Both reject the conclusions of Wolfgang Trilling, who, on the basis of linguistic, stylistic, structural, and theological evidence, regarded 2 Thessalonians as a pseudonymous writing. Both scholars viewed Trilling's evidence as being ambiguous, and Jewett noted with respect to the linguistic data assembled by Trilling: "Since he provides no exhaustive study of such features in other Pauline letters, we have no way of knowing whether variations in frequency are visible elsewhere, so it would appear that such marginal evidence carries weight only for someone who has already decided against Pauline authorship" (11; cf. Wanamaker, 23, 28). In short, linguistic features of 2 Thessalonians should not be compared only with 1 Thessalonians but with the language of the whole Pauline corpus.

Daryl Schmidt has taken up Jewett's challenge. On the basis of a computer program, produced by the GRAMCORD Institute, which has a grammatical concordance system for the Greek NT, he investigated those noun phrases (such as "the epiphany of his parousia," 2 Thess. 2:8, etc.; my trans.) that Trilling had noted. Schmidt's conclusion is that the frequency of Trilling's noun phrase strings in 2 Thessalonians separates it from the genuine Pauline epistles and places 2 Thessalonians in the company of Colossians and Ephesians. Schmidt reaches the same conclusion in his investigations of the frequency of coordinating conjunctions, (apart from "and"), frequency of adjectival constructions, and frequency of adverbs. Moreover, he demonstrated that the thanksgiving section of 2 Thess. 1:3-12 consists of "twenty-three sentence units, [namely] the matrix and twenty-two embedded sentences," while the thanksgiving sentence of Romans has five embeds, 1 Corinthians has six embeds, 2 Corinthians has five, but Ephesians has eighteen. Schmidt concludes: "The degree of syntactical complexity in the opening thanksgiving of 2 Thessalonians is unmatched elsewhere in the Pauline corpus and has its closest parallel in Ephesians and secondly in Colossians, two members of the Pauline corpus often considered 'pseud-epigraphic' " (in Collins, 385).

Since the pattern of distinctive stylistic features distinguishes 2 Thes-salonians from the authentic Pauline letters including 1 Thessalonians, and since the syntactical style of 2 Thessalonians is "closer to that of other disputed letters, Colossians and Ephesians" (ibid., 388), I can agree with Trilling and Schmidt that 2 Thessalonians was not written by Paul. Theo-logical differences between 2 Thessalonians and the other Pauline letters, especially 1 Thessalonians, undergird this conclusion, as we shall see.

During the summer of 1988 the Colloquium Biblicum Lovaniense fo-cused on 1 and 2 Thessalonians. Its papers were published subsequently: *The Thessalonian Correspondence.* Raymond F. Collins, the editor, com-mented: "one of the striking features of the colloquium was the nearly universal agreement as to the pseudepigraphal character" of 2 Thessalo-nians. This is not the impression one gets from reading the recent com-mentaries on 2 Thessalonians in English, but Collins's comment probably represents the way of the future.

Rhetorical Analysis

Rhetorical criticism for interpreting NT letters is one of the more recent developments. It has been employed, for instance, by Hans Dieter Betz in his commentary on Galatians and by George A. Kennedy in his important study on *New Testament Interpretation through Rhetorical Criticism.* Rob-ert Jewett, Frank Witt Hughes, and Glenn S. Holland used rhetorical criticism in their studies of 2 Thessalonians. Greco-Roman rhetorical hand-books discussed three kinds of rhetoric. *Judicial* rhetoric, practiced in law courts, endeavors to persuade an audience concerning right or wrong deeds committed in the past. *Deliberative* rhetoric seeks to persuade people, or an assembly, about the appropriateness of specific actions that would affect the future for good or ill of persons or assemblies. *Epideictic* rhetoric assigns blame or praise in the present on such occasions as honoring a benefactor, victory celebrations, political rallies, funerals, and the like. Jewett, Hughes, and Holland agree that 2 Thessalonians belongs to the deliberative genre of rhetoric in which the audience is confronted with choices affecting their future.

Second Thessalonians abounds in alternatives, antitheses, and choices that will affect the ultimate future of the addressees. The readers are told that those who now in steadfastness endure persecution will be vindicated and glorified, while their persecutors will suffer the punishment of eternal destruction (2 Thess. 1:4-12). Those who believe the author's testimony (1:10) are contrasted with those "who do not know God . . . and do not obey the gospel of our Lord Jesus" (1:8). The forged letter that caused confusion and alarm (2:2) is the antithesis of "our letter" (2:15), which contains the true "traditions" (2:15). The right apocalyptic timetable is the refutation of the false slogan that "the day of the Lord has come" (2:3-12; 2:2). The man of lawlessness, his "parousia" and deception (2:9), is the very opposite of the Lord Jesus Christ, who "will destroy him with the breath of his mouth" (2:8). Those to whom God sends "a powerful delusion" so that they "believe what is false" (2:11) are contrasted with the brothers and sisters whom God "chose from the beginning" (NRSV margin) for salvation "through belief in the truth" (2:13). The prayer that God would "comfort your hearts and strengthen them in every good work and word" (2:17) is the opposite of confused, unsettled minds caused by false doctrine (2:2). Finally, the disorderly who are unwilling to earn their own living are contrasted with the exemplary "Paul" who worked "night and day" and gave an example that must be imitated (3:6-15). If the addressees reject the false belief of the presence of the day of the Lord, if they obey the traditions as set forth by the author, if they avoid disorderly, lazy conduct, then their future is secure. If not, doom will befall them also, even as it will befall the persecutors of the elect (cf. Hughes, 76).

Rhetorical outlines of 2 Thessalonians as presented by Hughes, Holland, and Jewett are conveniently found in Jewett's book (225). Although there are some discrepancies between the outlines, their agreements are considerable. Having learned from each, here I modify them only slightly but pay greater attention to the arrangement within the diverse parts and among the parts.

Paul's letters, as well as 2 Thessalonians, were meant to be read to the community, or communities, and hence can be analyzed in terms of oral performance according to the pattern of rhetorical discourses of the Greco-Roman world. Part I of 2 Thessalonians, like many deliberate speeches, opens with an exordium (2 Thess. 1:1-12), which is an introduction. The exordium begins with the epistolary prescript (1:1-2), which identifies the author(s), who speaks with the authority of Paul. Next, the addressees who receive the customary salutation are identified. The "grace and peace" from God the Father and the Lord Jesus Christ (1:2) forms an inclusion with the wish prayers of 3:16, 18: "May the Lord of peace himself give you peace at all times in all ways"; "the grace of our Lord Jesus Christ be with all of you." Since Pauline letters were read or heard more than once the accent on grace and peace at the beginning and the end as well as the inclusive "at all times," "in all ways," and "all" can hardly be missed. The author wishes that confusion and discord in the community would cease in the present and the future through the power of divine peace and grace (see also the reference to grace in 1:12 at the conclusion of the exordium and at 2:16, the end of part II).

The next section of the exordium is a lengthy declaration, carefully structured, on the obligation of thanksgiving (1:3-12):

A) Thanksgiving for the Thessalonians' growth in faith and love and his boasting because of their steadfastness under persecution, 1:3-4

B) The apocalyptic retribution, 1:5-10

A') Paul's intercessory prayer on their behalf, 1:11-12

The focus of this thanksgiving lies in its center section, which is bracketed by prayer. The center section also contains an *aba'* pattern:

a) The apocalyptic reversal executed by God, 1:5-7a

b) The revelation of the Lord Jesus, 1:7b-8a

a') The apocalyptic reversal executed by Christ "on that day," 1:8b-10

This little letter of forty-seven verses contains a total of seventeen verses that refer to prayer. In terms of ancient rhetoric, prayers had great rhetorical value (Hughes, 52). In theological terms, this emphasis on prayer means that the author is aware that it is God in whose hands lies the beginning and the end of salvation. Furthermore, the thanksgiving section expresses not only solidarity between the author and the addressees, thus gaining their good will to listen to him; it also introduces the situation of persecution and oppression that the addressees face at present. Moreover, the exordium introduces the pertinent issue(s) with which the letter, or speech, will subsequently deal. In the center section of the thanksgiving (B, 1:5-10) the author sets forth the concept that their present experience of persecutions and afflictions is "evidence of the righteous judgment of God" that is to come, because their present afflictions will make them "worthy of the kingdom of God" (1:5). How is that so? Because suffering in history is God's discipline for his people (cf. Wisd. of Sol. 1:16—2:22; 11:9-10; 2 Macc. 6:12-16, etc.; cf. Bassler). Living in a sinful world of "wicked and evil people" (3:2), the faithful people of God must inevitably endure tribulation and persecution from the hands of those who "do not know God" and who "do not obey the gospel of our Lord Jesus" (1:8). Simultaneously it is God who through suffering disciplines his people in the present, so that they become "worthy" of his kingdom (1:5).

We do not know which form the persecutions and afflictions took. They could have ranged from verbal abuse to harassment, social ostracism, confiscation of property, imprisonment, and even worse. In the face of afflictions the author emphasized the necessity and propriety of giving thanks to God. Thanksgiving is hardly a person's normal response in a situation like that. But this author stated his reason for giving thanks to God. Their sufferings are not pointless because they are a means by which God enables them to be "worthy of the kingdom of God" (1:5) "on that day" when the great reversal shall occur through Christ's parousia (1:8-10). Obviously "that day" still lies in the future and equally obvious is that for the author the present afflictions (Greek *thlipsis*) are not signs of the presence of the day of the Lord. We may assume that the author's opponents who proclaimed that "the day of the Lord is already here" (2:2) interpreted the persecutions and afflictions as messianic woes that bring about, or are part of, the day of the Lord. (The notion of messianic woes has Jewish antecedents [see H. Schlier in *TDNT*, 3:145–46] and found expression in different NT writings [e.g., Mark 13:19, 24; 1 Pet. 4:12-13.]) Therefore the author consistently gave a different interpretation. The present tribulations are not eschatological messianic woes but evidence of the future apocalyptic reversal in which God's and Christ's just retribution will take place. Thus he contrasted present suffering with future glory. Then the faithful sufferers who have "believed" the author's "testimony" (1:10) will receive "rest" (RSV) from all hardships together with him (1:7).

But the emphasis in verses 6-10 lies on divine "vengeance" that will be poured out over the ungodly and result in their "eternal destruction," which is synonymous with being "separated from the presence of the Lord" Jesus Christ and from his majestic transforming glory (1:8-9; cf. Isa. 2:10, LXX) in which the believers will share (cf. 1:12). The synonymous parallelism of "those who do not know God and those who do not obey the gospel of our Lord Jesus" (1:8) in all probability does not refer to two distinct groups such as Gentiles and Jews. It apparently refers not just to the persecutors of the community but to a larger indefinite group that would also include the author's opponents. Instead of believing his "testimony" they have perverted it. They too do not "obey the gospel" nor hold fast to "the traditions" taught by Paul (cf. 1:10; 2:2-3a, 5, 15).

An intercessory prayer report (1:11-12) concludes the exordium. A synonymous parallelism indicates the content of the intercession: "that our God will make you worthy of his call [to salvation] and will fulfill by his power every good resolve and work of faith." The exordium introduces here the issue of "work," which is the topic of the exhortation of chapter 3. God is asked to act powerfully in the lives of the Thessalonians and to complete their good intention and their faithful work. For not all are faithful, as we hear later (3:2), and some refuse to work (3:6-12). The ultimate purpose of God's call and of his completing action in their lives is "that the name of our Lord Jesus may be glorified in you, and you in him" (1:12; cf. 2:14). All whom "the grace" of God will make worthy of his call will share in Christ's glory, even as their salvation, by grace, is the glorification of their Lord.

The Partitio, 2:1-2

The *partitio* in 2 Thessalonians lists the issues or propositions that are dealt with in the *probatio*. The first issue is the parousia of the Lord, which includes our being gathered with him and the false eschatology that announces "that the day of the Lord is already here." The section 2:3-12 constitutes the author's refutation of this false eschatology and is the first part of "the proof" (*probatio*). It is the most important section of this letter and the primary reason for its being written.

The second issue concerns the confusion (2:2a) within the community caused by the eschatological error; the section 2:13-16 seeks to reestablish personal firmness and doctrinal soundness, "belief in the truth" (2:13). This section contains the second part of his "proof" (Hughes, 57).

Moreover, the *partitio* deals with three possible sources that gave rise to the oracle that "the day of the Lord is already here." The origin of this erroneous announcement could be the pronouncement of a "spirit"-inspired prophet; it could be the result of a "word," that is, an oral teaching, perhaps even attributed to Paul; or it could be based on "a letter purporting to be from us" (RSV). The author will state the sources of sound doctrine in 2:5 and 2:15. They do not include "spirit"-inspired prophecy (cf. 1 Thess. 5:19).

Glenn Holland has argued that we must distinguish the "day" of the Lord Jesus, which commences with his parousia, from the "day of the Lord" God, which is a day of wrath. In 2 Thess. 2:9-12 "the appearance of the antagonist" (the lawless one of 2:9) is the central event of "the day of the Lord, the day of wrath" (Holland, 119). This distinction does not commend itself. The exordium had already spoken of the revelation of the *Lord* Jesus on *that day*, and the *partitio* clearly identifies the "coming of our Lord Jesus Christ" as the "day of the Lord" (2:1-2). Finally, the author did not specify that the appearance of the lawless one constitutes the presence of the day of the Lord. Such a specification would have been necessary if he had thought that the appearance of the antagonist is "the central event of the day of the Lord." There is no evidence that Paul, or the author of 2 Thessalonians, or his opponents distinguished between two different days of the Lord. Certainly for Paul, as well as for the author of 2 Thessalonians, the day of the Lord and the parousia of Christ are identical (cf. 1 Thess. 4:15; 5:1-2).

What then did the perpetrators of the oracle concerning the presence of the "day of the Lord" mean? The most likely answer is that for them the parousia of Christ has already taken place secretly and therefore "the day of the Lord is already here" (cf. Jewett, 100). Of course, the day of the Lord is not a twenty-four-hour day but a new epoch that, according to the perpetrators of the slogan of 2:2, has already been ushered in through the messianic woes, the tribulations, experienced in the present. It may be that they interpreted a text like 1 Thess. 2:16 (the wrath of God has come upon the Jews at last) as the beginning of the final judgment and connected with a particular calamity, such as the destruction of Jerusalem. But basic to the notion of the presence of "the day of the Lord" is the parousia of Christ, a notion that the opponents of the Thessalonians seemed to have affirmed.

But is this view probable? Gerhard Friedrich has conveniently assembled the material from Josephus about Jewish messianic prophets (*TDNT*, 6:826–27). Moreover, the Synoptic apocalypses warn not only against false prophets but also against false Christs who proclaim in Jesus' name: "I am he!" (Mark 13:6; cf. 13:21-22), "I am the Christ" (Matt. 24:5). Luke 21:8 reads: "many will come in my name and say, 'I am he!' and, 'The time is near [*ho kairos engiken*].' " These texts seem to indicate that there were indeed people who claimed to be Jesus, returned to earth. The oracle of 2 Thess. 2:2 must be seen within the general context of the apocalyptic fever that gripped segments of Judaism and Christianity during the last three or four decades of the first century A.D. The Synoptic apocalypses, each in their own way, as well as 2 Thessalonians argue against the apocalyptic deception that Jesus has returned, that "the day of the Lord is already here." "Let no one deceive you" (2 Thess. 2:3a), "beware that no one leads you astray" (Mark 13:5).

The Probatio, 2:3-16

Hughes divides the proof into two parts (57). In the first part (2:3-12) the author refutes the apocalyptic deception about the presence of the day of the Lord. He constructed an apocalyptic timetable that proves that the day of the Lord could not possibly have arrived already. The purpose of this timetable is not to determine the day and the hour of Christ's parousia, as Luther's follower Michael Stifel did when he calculated that the parousia would occur on October 19, 1533, 8 A.M. sharp. For Johann Albrecht Bengel (1687–1752) it was to be on June 18, 1836. The purpose of the timetable in 2 Thessalonians 2 was to create a distance between the present time and the parousia of the Lord and thus prove the error of those who announced "that the day of the Lord is already here."

The structure of this section is:

A) The apostasy and the man of lawlessness, 2:3b-5
B) The present as the time of the *katechon* (neuter) and of the mystery of lawlessness, 2:6-7a
B′) The removal of the *katechōn* (masculine) in the future, 2:7b

A') The parousia and destruction of the lawless one; his deception of unbelievers according to the will of God, 2:8-12

The focus of this section lies in verses 6-7 (B and B'), which are anything but clear. They are written in a deliberately mysterious and mystifying manner. In verse 6 the NRSV translates: "what is now restraining *him*" (Greek *to katechon*), but the pronoun "him" is not in the Greek text, and the translation of the participle with "restraining" and "the one who restrains" (Greek *ho katechōn*, v. 7; again the pronoun "him" is absent from the Greek text) is a matter of interpretation. We may never find a solution to these two verses that is generally acceptable.

Commentaries list a great variety of interpretations of the *katechon*. Space permits me to refer briefly to only one. Agreeing with Strobel, Trilling in his excellent commentary on 2 Thessalonians suggests that the concept of the *katechon* in 2:6-7 is a technical term for the delay of the parousia according to the plan of God. There is no real difference between the masculine and the neuter form of this participle. Behind the *katechon* stands God himself, who delays the end and prevents, for the time being, the appearance of the lawless one (Trilling, 92). This interpretation is improbable.

In verse 5 the author reminded the addressees that Paul told (imperfect) them this apocalyptic timetable in the past, while he was still with them. Verse 6 is literally: "And now [in the present] you know [that is, you experience] the *katechon*." What the addressees experience in the present is persecution and tribulation (1:4-7). It seems to me that the *katechon*, because it (he) is effective in the present time, should be related to the present experience of tribulations. Moreover, according to verse 7, "the mystery of lawlessness" (i.e., a secret rebellion against God, known only to believers) is also operative in the present. Furthermore, the verb *katechein* has an unusual breadth of meaning and can be used in a benevolent sense or in a hostile sense (e.g., to have a legal claim—or an improper claim— upon a person, to rule, to lay hold of, to possess, to arrest, to seize, to oppress, to suppress, to detain, to restrain, to prevail). In a hostile sense this verb is used in verse 6 either as a veiled, deliberately mysterious reference to their present experience of tribulations or as an ironic reference. In the latter case the author was aware that pagan magistrates justified their anti-Christian activity with precisely the same verb. To them it meant "restraining" the Christians with their abominable superstition. The Christians viewed such restraint as oppression, or as the prevailing of the secret rebellion against God by a pagan society and its head, who is *ho katechōn* (v. 7). I paraphrase verse 6: "And now, in the present, you experience the restraining-oppressing power." This present restraining and oppression of

Christians lasts until the revelation of the "man of lawlessness," and thus it distinguishes the present from the future. Equally important is the fact that the author does not relate the present tribulations to the ultimate future, which is the day of the Lord, or the parousia of Christ. Instead he relates them to the penultimate future, which is the revelation of "the lawless one."

In verse 7 the author indicates the hidden connection between the present and the penultimate future. "For the mystery of lawlessness is already at work" and believers know it because they experience it, even though their oppressors are unaware of this "mystery." They would be scandalized to hear that in the opinion of this author lawlessness and rebellion against God are secretly at work among them and through them, especially since Roman ideology valued law and order and peace. The present force of lawlessness will come to a climax in the revelation of the lawless one (v. 8a), but this will happen only when the prior figure of *ho katechōn* has departed from the scene of history and is "removed" according to God's timetable. The masculine form of *katechōn* in verse 7 appears to be an ad hoc formulation by the author on the basis of the *katechon* (neuter) of verse 6 and is a deliberately veiled reference to the persecutor, be it magistrate, governor, or emperor. His removal signals the next stage in the apocalyptic drama.

From the perspective of apocalyptic theology, the empire and its magistrates do not appear as God's servants for good, restraining and punishing evil and praising good conduct (Rom. 13:1-5). Instead the empire's representatives are the religious-political power of secret lawlessness that arrests and seizes, impounds and confiscates, restrains and oppresses, and in so doing causes tribulations to believers in the present. The verb *katechein* is sufficiently broad to cover diverse forms of chicanery experienced by Christians. The author would like his readers to understand that the activity of the *katechon* signifies neither the presence of the day of the Lord nor the presence of the ultimate evil in history. History prior to the day of the Lord has two distinct periods. Both are represented by nameless figures, the *katechōn* (v. 7) and the *anomos* (v. 8)—the second will not appear until the first is removed (v. 7).

Like the parousia of a Roman emperor visiting a province, the appearance of the "lawless one" will be a public event and a parody of Christ's parousia. As the agent of Satan the "lawless one" will deceive "those who are perishing" with displays of power, signs, and wonders (vv. 9-10). All evil, all deception, and all self-deification will be embodied in him. He will take his "seat in the temple of God [cf. Dan. 9:27; 11:31, 36; 12:11; Mark 13:14], declaring himself to be God" (2 Thess. 2:4). It is worth noting that in distinction to other antagonists in Jewish and Christian tradition, the "lawless one" of 2 Thessalonians is not described in terms of persecuting the people of God (cf. Revelation 13). He is a deceiver rather than a persecutor, a satanic miracle worker rather than one "drunk with the blood of the saints" (Rev. 17:6). The reason for this picture of the "lawless one" is not hard to find. Since the Thessalonians are already experiencing persecution, the author would hardly give them consolation and calm their unsettled minds if he were then to tell them that their present sufferings are but a prelude to greater afflictions yet to come. "Let no one deceive you," the author had warned at the beginning of this section (2 Thess. 2:3). The deception caused by an erroneous eschatology is completed with finality in the deception wrought by the "lawless one" upon those "who are perishing, because they refused to love the truth and so be saved" (v. 10).

Simultaneously, God's purpose is worked out even through the antagonist's activity. The great deceiver at the end of history is also an agent of God's wrath. To those who refuse to believe the truth, "God sends them a powerful delusion [cf. Ezek. 14:9], leading them to believe" the great lie (v. 11); thus they are condemned. Having rejected the gospel, the truth, which includes the right apocalyptic timetable, they take "pleasure in wickedness" (v. 12). Those who do not believe will not believe, because God surrenders them to a "powerful delusion" (cf. Rom. 1:24-25). Human responsibility and divine all-encompassing activity cannot be balanced on the same ledger but must remain in tension. Before God we cannot blame him for our unbelief and delusions, nor can we deny his all-embracing power. "Does evil befall a city, unless the Lord has done it?" (Amos 3:6, RSV); "I form light and create darkness, I make weal and create woe" (Isa. 45:7). God works all in all, good and evil, life and death, creation and destruction. Within his will all things occur.

The apocalyptic scenario reaches its climactic conclusion on the day of the Lord. Then, at his parousia, "the Lord Jesus will destroy" the Antichrist with "the breath of his mouth" (2 Thess. 2:8b). The fate of his minions need not be repeated because it had already been depicted in 1:5-10.

The importance of this apocalyptic timetable is fivefold. First, it proves that the oracle of 2:2 is wrong. Second, it creates an indefinite distance between the present and the day of the Lord by inserting two intermediate stages—the removal of the *katechon* and the appearance of the lawless one. Third, it views the present experience of suffering in a new perspective as the activity of the *katechon*, not as messianic woes. Fourth, it guards believers against the future deception by "the lawless one." Fifth, it assures them that God is in control. In linear form the apocalyptic timetable is: (1) the present (vv. 6a and 7a); (2) the future removal of the *katechon* (7b); (3) the parousia of the "lawless one"; and the deception/rebellion (vv. 3-4, 8a, 9-10); (4) the parousia of Christ and the destruction of the "lawless one" (v. 8b).

According to Hughes (57), the second half of the proof (2:13-17) deals with counteracting the confusion caused by the false eschatology of 2:2. What better way to restore mental and spiritual stability than prayer and exhortation! In 2:15 we hear the first explicit imperative after the warning of 2:3a. The structure is:

A) Obligation of thanksgiving, 2:13-14
B) Exhortation, 2:15
A') Wish prayer, 2:16-17

In sharp contrast to those who did not believe the truth and will be condemned (2:10-12), the author is obligated to give thanks for his sisters and brothers, because God chose them for salvation "from the beginning" (v. 13, NRSV margin; cf. Eph. 1:4). The means by which they reach salvation is the "sanctification of [their] spirit and belief in the truth" (my trans.). One could translate differently: "sanctification by the [Holy] Spirit" (NRSV), but since the Holy Spirit is not mentioned in this letter otherwise, it may be better to choose the former translation. The issue is mental, spiritual, and doctrinal stability in place of confusion.

God "called" the Thessalonians when Paul preached the gospel to them, and the goal of God's call, the author assures them, is obtaining "the glory of our Lord Jesus Christ" (v. 14; cf. Rom. 8:17; 1 Cor. 15:43; 2 Cor. 3:18; Phil. 3:21). To obtain Christ's glory is to receive a resurrection life the same as his, to be transformed by and into the form of existence that Christ now has with the brilliance of God radiating from him to the believers and from them to him (cf. 2 Thess. 1:10, 12). In short, "our being gathered together to him" (2:1) entails salvation in terms of glorification of the believers, and for this salvation the author thanks God and by it he assures his readers.

The explicit exhortation of 2:15 is the focus of this part of the proof. "So then, brothers and sisters, stand firm," instead of "being quickly shaken in mind or alarmed" (2:2). "Hold fast to the traditions [plural, including the timetable, but also traditions regarding orderly conduct and work; cf. 3:6, 10] that you were taught by us either by word of mouth [cf. 2:5] or by our letter." The reference to "our letter" (singular) draws a contrast to the letter "purporting to be from us" (2:2, RSV), which is a forgery, even as his oral teaching of verses 5 and 15 is contrasted with "the word," as from us. Paul had never said that the day of the Lord had come, but from the beginning he had consistently taught an apocalyptic timetable (2:5). Most interpreters see a reference to 1 Thessalonians in the phrase "our letter." But this view is probably not right. One would expect a plural, "our letters," namely 1 and 2 Thessalonians. Hence "our letter" probably refers to 2 Thessalonians only.

Instead of interpreting the wish prayer of 2:16 as *peroratio*, as Hughes does, I see in it a rhetorical inclusion with the thanksgiving of 2:13-14. The opening of the wish prayer is also repeated in 3:16 (*autos de ho kyrios*) at the end of the exhortation section and forms an inclusion with the prayer of 3:5. Here in 2:16 the author expresses his solidarity with his readers by telling them that Christ and God "loved *us* and through grace gave *us* eternal comfort and good hope." Such comfort and hope result not only from their election and call (2:13-14) but also from the apocalyptic timetable that he had just repeated for them. His two petitions ask God to comfort (or encourage) their hearts, their inner selves, in the face of the pressures they endure and to strengthen them in their outward conduct in "every good work and word."

Exhortatio, 3:1-12 and Peroratio, 3:13-18

Transition, 3:1-5. Most commentators see the signal for the beginning of the exhortation section in the phrase "Finally, brothers" (Greek *to loipon . . . adelphoi*). In 1 Thess. 4:1 *loipon* (without the article) indicates the beginning of the concluding section, and the same holds true for Phil. 4:8, etc., but not for 2 Tim. 4:8 or 1 Cor. 7:29, where it is used inferentially ("therefore"; cf. BAGD, 480). The previous wish prayer concluded in 2:17 by stating that God should "*strengthen* them in every good work and *word.*" Because strengthening them in every good *word* implies that God's word, as preached by Paul, would triumph in their lives, therefore we now hear a request for intercessory prayer (3:1): "that the *word* of the Lord may speed on and triumph everywhere, just as it is among you." Moreover, the promise that the faithful God "will strengthen you and guard you from evil" (3:3, NRSV margin; or "from the evil one," NRSV) recasts themes of 2:13-17. The prayer wish of 3:5 recalls 2:17. In short, one could easily understand 3:1-5 as concluding the *probatio* and translate *to loipon* with "therefore." Jewett (80) and I, in the previous edition of this commentary, did just that.

But I must admit that generally *to loipon* should be translated with "finally," indicating the beginning of a new section. Moreover, the author's model, 1 Thessalonians, uses it this way in 4:1, and a new note is struck in the injunction "we command," found in 2 Thess. 3:4 and repeated in 3:6 and 12 (cf. "obey" in 3:14). But even though 3:1-5 opens the exhortation section it functions as a transition to the following exhortations.

Having prayed for the Thessalonians (2:16-17), the author now asks them to pray for him (3:1). Reciprocal prayers express the church's unity between the missionary-preacher and his people. Paul himself had requested intercessory prayers at the end of some of his letters (Rom. 15:20; 1 Thess.

5:25). Col. 4:3 and Eph. 6:19 contain the same request. The twofold content of their intercessions should be: (1) that the "word of the Lord may spread rapidly and gloriously" (literally, "may run and be glorified"); and (2) that the author and his coworkers "may be delivered from *the* wicked and evil people, for not all are faithful [literally, 'faith is not of all']" (my trans.). The definite article in front of "wicked and evil people" suggests that the author has a specific group in mind. Perhaps he is referring to heretics who are unfaithful to the tradition and upset the believers. The unfaithful are contrasted not with true believers but with the faithful God and the promise that he "will strengthen you and guard you from evil" (or "the evil one," who operates in the present via the *katechon* in "the mystery of lawlessness"; 2:7). In 2:17 the strengthening implies adherence to the apocalyptic tradition transmitted by the author (cf. 2:15). The hearers are secure from evil insofar as they keep the traditions and thus do "the things that we command" (3:4; cf. 3:6).

Having asked for intercession at the beginning, the author now closes his transition with a wish prayer (3:5). "The love of God" to which "the Lord" (Jesus) should direct their hearts is probably a subjective genitive, meaning God's love toward the readers, rather than their love toward God (cf. 2:16). If so, then "steadfastness of Christ" should also be interpreted as a subjective genitive, meaning Christ's perseverance under trials and tribulations as motivation for conduct. But apart from the fact that Christ does not appear as motivation for conduct in this letter, this interpretation has the additional difficulty that the prayer addressed to the Lord Jesus himself would now ask him to direct their hearts to his own steadfastness. This reading is possible, but it would be unusual. In terms of objective genitives the wish prayer would ask the *Lord* (Jesus) to direct their hearts to love toward *God* and to the patient expectation of Christ, that is, of Christ's parousia (cf. 1:4; thus von Dobschütz's interpretation). In either case there are difficulties.

In the exhortation proper we twice find the phrase "we command you" (or "such persons") in the (name of the) Lord, 3:6 and 12. Sandwiched in between is the example of Paul, who earned his own living (3:7-10). From a rhetorical point of view verses 13-18 seem to function as a peroration, introduced by a new address: "but you, brothers" (v. 13, my trans.). The wish prayer (at v. 16) balances the wish prayer of 3:5 at the beginning. Thus I arrive at the following structure:

A) Transition, 3:1-5:

      a) *Exhortation* for intercessory *prayer*, 3:1-3

      b) Confidence concerning the *obedience* of his hearers, 3:4

      a') Wish *prayer*, 3:5

B) Command to keep away from the disorderly, 3:6
C) The example of Paul, 3:7-10
B') Command to the disorderly, 3:11-12
A') *Peroratio*, including epistolary postscript, 3:13-18:
      a) *Exhortation* to do good, 3:13
      b) Dealing with the *disobedient*, 3:14-15
      a') Wish *prayer* and epistolary postscript, 3:16-18

Exhortatio, 3:6-12.   The first command is addressed to the obedient members of the community (3:6). The author commands them in the strongest possible form, namely, "in the name of our Lord Jesus Christ," whose authority undergirds the author's command and makes it absolute. To reject his command is to reject the Lord: "keep away from believers [that is, 'from any brother' and sister] who are living in disorderly fashion and not according to the tradition that they [some manuscripts read 'you'] received" (v. 6, my trans.). The disorderly are clearly identified later on as those Christians who are unwilling to work and therefore unable to provide for their own livelihood. Hence these lazy Christians live off the rest of the community and its more prosperous members.

The "tradition" that the disorderly had received but ignored consists of two items: first, the "example" of Paul, whom all members of the community "ought to imitate" (vv. 7 and 9; cf. 1 Thess. 4:1; 1:6; 2:14; 1 Cor. 4:16; 11:1; Phil. 3:17; 4:9). Far from being disorderly and lazy, eating "anyone's bread without paying" (2 Thess. 3:8), Paul set an obligatory example when he was with them. He worked long hours, both "night and day" (cf. 1 Thess. 2:9), "with toil and labor" so that he could be self-sufficient with respect to his needs and not be a burden to anyone (cf. 1 Cor. 9:3-18; 2 Cor. 11:7, 9; Acts 18:1-3). To use oneself as an example was a convention of Greco-Roman moralists. Personal examples "were regarded as more persuasive than words and as providing concrete models to imitate" (Malherbe, 135). Paul's example was to be a visual aid in teaching self-sufficiency, not being a burden to members of the community. His example is one part of the tradition that the disorderly had received.

The second part consisted of oral teaching (2 Thess. 3:10). "When we were with you" Paul used to teach (imperfect) them not only the correct apocalyptic timetable (2:5), but he gave this command repeatedly (imperfect) as a community rule: "Anyone unwilling to work should not eat" at the expense of the community. This command does not apply to persons who cannot find work (cf. Matt. 20:7a), nor does it refer to old people, the sick, maimed, blind, and lame who can no longer work. It refers only to those who are able but unwilling to work. In short, Paul's example as well as his explicit teaching are warrants for discontinuing the support of the disorderly who are "not busy; they are busybodies" (NIV, which reproduces the Greek wordplay of *ergazomenoi* and *periergazomenoi*). The busybodies are meddlers who interfere in other people's temporal and/or spiritual affairs but are unwilling to work for their own living.

They are now addressed directly (v. 12) and commanded, by divine authority, "in the Lord Jesus Christ to do their work quietly and to earn their own living" and in so doing live in accord with the tradition that specifies the obligation of imitating the example of Paul and of obeying the community rule taught by Paul. Verse 12 seeks to alter their behavior. Changing behavior is a function of deliberative rhetoric. This verse forms an inclusion with verse 6, which seeks to alter the behavior of the disobedient.

At this point one may ask whether the disorderliness warned against in chapter 3 was caused by the false eschatology of 2:2. The author does not explicitly connect the two problems, and therefore some commentators reject any linkage between disorderliness and apocalyptic enthusiasm in this letter (e.g., Wanamaker, 162–63; Russell, 109–10). But if such a connection was obvious to the author as well as to the addressees, he had no reason to make that linkage explicit. Moreover, the catchwords "faithful *work*" (my trans.) and "good *work*" had been introduced in the exordium and at the end of the second half of the proof (1:11; 2:17). Finally, if the Greek phrase *hypomonē tou Christou* in 3:5 does not mean "Christ's steadfastness," or "endurance, fortitude, that comes from communion with Christ," but rather, as is probable, "patient expectation of Christ," that is, of his parousia, then a connection does exist between the disorderliness of 3:6-12 and the confusion concerning the presence of the eschaton in 2:2. One must also realize that, in general, false beliefs have ethical consequences. Therefore it is probable that the failure of some (or of many) Christians to continue their daily work was caused by their belief in the presence of the eschaton. Why work, if the Lord has already come in secret? His parousia signals the imminent transformation of the world from a vale of toil and tears into a new paradise (cf. *2 Bar.* 29:5-8; 73:1—74:2, etc.) If so, the disorderly could afford to disregard the old order as being passé, and their unwillingness to work was an expression of their faith in the presence of Christ's parousia. For the author their conduct was contrary to the tradition of the apocalyptic timetable that Paul had repeatedly communicated while he was with them and is contrary to his example and the instruction that he had repeatedly given (2:5, 15; 3:6, 9-10).

Peroratio, Including Epistolary Postscript, 3:13-18.   A *peroratio* should appear at the end of a speech, summarize the chief point or points, and excite indignation or sympathy for a particular point of view. Different commentators come to differing conclusions about the *peroratio* (see the convenient chart 6 in Jewett, 225). I hold that the *peroratio* begins at 3:13 and ends with the epistolary conclusion in 3:18. The author used the vocative "brothers and sisters" seven times, each time to signal a new section or an important subsection (1:3; 2:1, 13, 15 ["hold fast to the traditions that you were taught by us, either by word of mouth or by our letter"]; 3:1, 6, 13). It therefore seems unlikely that in this carefully structured letter or speech 3:13 would not introduce a new section or subsection, especially since beginning with 3:13 the issues are summarized. "Brothers and sisters, do not be weary in doing what is right" recalls the "faithful work" and the "good work" of 1:11 and 2:17, as well as the exhortation to "work" for self-suffiency, 3:6-11.

Next, the author attacks a particular group with a community rule. "Take note of those who do not obey what we say *in this letter*" (v. 14). This group certainly includes both the disorderly of 3:6-12 and those who proclaim the presence of the day of the Lord (2:2). "Have nothing to do with them" recalls 3:6 but now applies equally to those who as "busybodies" are involved in promulgating the false apocalyptic timetable of 2:2. Yet, surprisingly, the author exhorts: "Do not regard them as enemies, but warn them as [because they are] believers." The problem of heresy and improper conduct receives an evangelical answer. On the one hand, the community must draw a boundary. Therefore the exhortation to keep away from them (3:6) and have nothing to do with them (3:14) indicates that their false eschatology (2:2) *and* their disorderly life-style are not acceptable alternatives to the tradition that the community received (2:15; 3:6, 9, 10). There must be clear boundaries. On the other hand, the exhortation not to look at Christians who hold erroneous doctrine and practice as enemies but to warn them because they are brothers and sisters (3:15) expresses the purpose and goal of an evangelical church discipline, which is to win back the erring brother/sister for life within the community.

Therefore the epistolary postscript is bracketed by a wish prayer (v. 16) and by a benediction (v. 18), both of which emphasize *all*: "at *all* times, in *all* ways" (v. 16); "the Lord be with *all* of you" (v. 16); "the grace of our Lord Jesus Christ be with *all* of you" (v. 18). The author hopes that in spite of the failure of Paul's oral instruction when he was with them (2:5; 3:10), his letter, 2 Thessalonians, would restore the erring sisters and brothers to the unity of the community.

The epistolary postscript of 3:17 authenticates this letter as a genuine and authoritative written communication by Paul. The "mark" of authenticity "in every letter of mine" is to distinguish this letter from a forgery (cf. 2:2). The mark of authenticity is the greeting in his own handwriting, namely, the wish prayer of "peace" in verse 16 and the benediction of "grace" in verse 18. He adds, "it is the way I write." They can check his handwriting and find that 1 Thessalonians does not have it (1 Thess. 5:27 notwithstanding). In some letters (rather than in every one) Paul wrote the concluding words himself (1 Cor. 16:21; Gal. 6:11; Philem. 19; cf. Col. 4:18), but never in order to authenticate his letter and distinguish it from forgeries.

Concluding Comments

Glenn Holland has conveniently laid out and thoroughly discussed the use of 1 Thessalonians by the author of 2 Thessalonians (8–33 and 59–90). Besides the similarity in structure (e.g., two thanksgivings), in vocabulary, and in formulaic phrases, one finds striking differences in style. More important is the fact that the author of 2 Thessalonians nowhere explicitly referred to the eschatology of 1 Thess. 4:13-17 in order to combat the false eschatology of those who advocate the presence of the day of the Lord. Instead he substituted an apocalyptic timetable that creates a distance between the present and Christ's parousia by setting forth two intervening factors of indeterminable length: the disappearance of the *katechon* and the appearance of the lawless one, his entrance into the temple, and the apostasy caused by him.

Clearly in 1 Thess. 5:1-3 there can be no "signs" prior to the day of the Lord, and the believers are already now children of light, sons and daughters of the day, equipped with God's armor of faith, love, and hope (1 Thess. 5:4-8; cf. Rom. 13:11). In 2 Thess. 2:5, however, we hear that Paul himself had taught this timetable repeatedly when he established the community in Thessalonica. This statement is historically most improbable, as improbable as it would be to argue that Luther sold indulgences in Wittenberg on Sunday morning and preached on Romans in the afternoon. In short, the pseudonymous author of 2 Thessalonians meant his timetable to be a substitute for the eschatology of Paul as expressed in 1 Thessalonians 4 and 5. He writes under the name of Paul in order to negate Paul's eschatology.

It is quite probable that the author went one further step and suggested that 1 Thessalonians is a forgery. On the one hand he imitated the structure and language of 1 Thessalonians. On the other hand he never referred to it. Contrary to Jewett (186) and others, 2 Thess. 2:15 does not refer to 1 Thessalonians. "Our letter" refers to 2 Thessalonians, otherwise one would expect "letters" (plural). Moreover, an apocalyptic timetable is not even taught in 1 Thessalonians—indeed, it is excluded. In 2 Thess. 2:15 the author admonished his readers to hold to "the traditions that you were taught by us, either by word [of mouth when Paul was with them; 2:5] or by *our* letter." The heretical eschatology mentioned in 2:2 also claimed a Pauline letter as its basis, and that letter in all probability was 1 Thessalonians. If so, the author seems to suggest that 1 Thessalonians is a forgery, a "letter purporting to be from us" (2:2, RSV). At any rate, according to the author the oracle concerning the presence of the day of the Lord cannot claim to be based on a genuine letter of Paul. Also, the mark of authenticity in 3:17 seems to suggest that 1 Thessalonians is to be viewed as a forgery, because obviously 1 Thessalonians does not have such a mark. If so, the pseudonymous letter, 2 Thessalonians, seeks to be accepted as the one and only legitimate letter to the Thessalonians (cf. Lindemann, Laub, Hughes).

As 2 Thess. 2:2 indicates, the letter was written at a time of apocalyptic fever and fervor, when some announced that Christ's parousia had already taken place, apparently in secret (cf. Mark 13:6, 22). Others told of the opening of tombs and the raising of the bodies of many saints and their appearance in the holy city (Matt. 27:52-53, which also contains Matthew's reinterpretation). The author endeavored to counteract the proclamation by apocalyptic Paulinists that Christ had already returned to earth and that his new order was being (secretly) realized. He substituted a timetable for Paul's eschatology in order to prove that this proclamation was not so. With his substitution, he in fact also refuted Pauline eschatology (Hughes, 84–86). Since the apocalyptic Paulinists probably undergirded their preaching by making use of 1 Thessalonians, the author probably suggested that his own letter (2 Thessalonians) is the real letter of Paul to the Thessalonians. Finally, he admonished all to a life-style of sober-mindedness and self-sufficiency, modeled on the exemplary Paul.

The present lectionaries of Episcopalians, Lutherans, Methodists, Presbyterians, and Roman Catholics do not contain 2 Thess. 2:3-12 among the lessons for Sundays in the three-year cycle. There are lessons from chapter 1 and others beginning with 2:13, and all five denominations use 3:6-13 (or 3:7-12) on the twenty-sixth Sunday after Pentecost in cycle C. But the very heart of 2 Thessalonians and the reason for the writing of this letter—2:3-12—is conspicuous by its absence in the lectionaries for the Sunday lessons. The reason for this absence is not difficult to surmise. What is a present-day preacher to say after reading an apocalyptic timetable on Sunday morning? It reads like prophecy about historical events to come, but they have not come about. True enough. But the preacher faces essentially the same problem when he or she has to deal with Paul's imminent-end expectation, which remained constant from 1 Thess. 4:13-17 to his last letter, Rom. 13:11-12, or when the appointed Gospel reading is one of the apocalyptic texts of the Synoptics. A few concluding remarks are meant to set some parameters.

First, Christian faith is grounded in the past act of Jesus' salvific death and resurrection; we *believe* his saving work (he "was handed over to death for our trespasses and was raised for our justification," Rom. 4:25); we *confess* the person of Jesus, as Lord (1 Cor. 12:3; Messiah and son of God, Matt. 16:16, etc.). We *await* his parousia. The future hope is not the basis or content of faith but an interpretation of the future in the light of the resurrection.

Second, although Christian faith can be transmitted in creedal formulas, such as 1 Cor. 15:3-5, Christian *hope* cannot be transmitted this way, because we ourselves are part of the stream of time. Therefore Luke changed Mark 13 in his apocalyptic section (Luke 21), and the author of 2 Thessalonians did the same with Paul's eschatology. I can illustrate this point briefly. The statement that the Lord's parousia is near, temporally imminent, can, of course, be repeated for a millennium or two, but already a hundred years after it was first uttered it has changed its force. Although this statement originally expressed a fervent hope that impinged upon lives, giving them comfort and strength, this statement changes as time passes into something that is also affirmed in spite of the fact that the Lord has not come. The words may still be the same, but the original force and meaning have changed. His nearness can also be reinterpreted in terms of his hidden presence among the two or three gathered in his name. This reinterpretation is complete in John's Gospel. But I must emphasize that the famous "delay" of the parousia did not cause a crisis of faith, because Christian faith is grounded in the past act of Christ's death and resurrection, not in the hope of the future.

Third, Christians hope in the light of the resurrection that evil will not be rampant in all eternity and that there will be a vindication of righteous sufferers (2 Thess. 1:10), because there was a vindication of the Righteous Sufferer, Jesus, our Lord.

Fourth, over against ancient and modern apocalyptic fanatics, the author of 2 Thessalonians (with his admittedly out-of-date timetable) cooled the temper of apocalyptic enthusiasm by distancing the present from the ultimate end. In chapter 3 he rebuked the "disorderly" and pointed to "work" to be done on earth.

Fifth, the author saw evil operating in his present time, in political institutions. It was not the ultimate evil but a foretaste of it, the "mystery of lawlessness," which I have interpreted as lawlessness operating in a secret, hidden manner. It may be helpful for flag-waving Christians to be admonished to be more critical in their political enthusiasm. Simultaneously, others may be helped to appreciate the relative goodness of a government that grants freedom of religion, opposes religious persecution, and seeks, however imperfectly, to do what is right.

Finally, 2 Thessalonians may help us to celebrate the theological diversity of the NT in which writings such as 1 and 2 Thessalonians, Romans and James, the Gospel of John and the Revelation to John exist side by side, held together not by the glue of the bookbinder but by the symphony of a pluriform, at times seemingly contradictory, witness to God and his Anointed. To him be glory forever, and "the grace of our Lord Jesus Christ be with all of you" (2 Thess. 3:18).

1–2 TIMOTHY, TITUS

Introduction

The Pastoral Epistles (1 Timothy, 2 Timothy, and Titus) are controversial letters, whose interpretation is much disputed. Some scholars understand them as "early catholic," a label that connotes overinstitutionalization, subordination of the Word to an office, and quenching of the Spirit. Others understand the letters as representing the inevitable institutionalization of Christianity, which, indeed, preserves the Word. Thus, some interpreters hail the Pastorals for their protection of the truth. Others vilify them for a rigid structure of offices. Some scholars protest the denigration of women evident in the letters. Others identify in them protection for women in a sexist society. A long-standing interpretation charges the Pastorals with negative accommodation to the world. A more recent look at the letters argues that they have a sophisticated program for mature Christian life in society. Scholarship on the Pastoral Epistles is obviously far from unified in its understanding of the three letters.

The basic situations reflected in the letters are clear, whether placed in the life of historical Paul or fictive (i.e., a fictional construct around which the author structures his thoughts).[1] Timothy and Titus, to whom the letters are addressed, were representatives of Paul. Timothy had responsibility for the churches in Ephesus, and Titus had similar duties on the island of Crete. In Titus the directive is expressly stated: "I left you behind in Crete for this reason, so that you should put in order what remained to be done, and should appoint elders in every town, as I directed you" (1:5). Paul was planning to spend the winter in the Greek city of Nicopolis and hoped that Titus would be able to join him there (3:12). In 1 Timothy Paul repeats an admonition to Timothy to continue to work in Ephesus because of the danger of false teachings (1 Tim. 1:3-4). Timothy is also directed to pay attention to organizational details, although the impression is that the church was more thoroughly organized in Ephesus than in Crete (1 Tim. 3:1-13; 5:17-22) Timothy was working with existing structures, whereas Titus needed to create them. Paul hoped to come to Timothy soon, although the apostle was aware that he might be delayed (1 Tim. 3:14-15). While addressed to individuals, Titus and 1 Timothy are rather formal and appear to be meant for a wider audience.

Second Timothy has little interest in church structure (although it contains many insights on ministry) and is more personal than the other two letters. Paul is a prisoner (1:8) in chains (1:16; 2:9), apparently in Rome (1:17). Various Christians have deserted him (1:15; 4:10), but he longs to see Timothy (1:4) and hopes that Timothy will soon be able to join him (4:9). He has already faced one legal proceeding, from which the Lord rescued him (4:16-17), but anticipates that he is near the end of his life. His fight and race are almost over, and he looks forward to eternal reward (4:6-8, 18).

These three letters have been understood since antiquity as constituting a unit, since their vocabulary, writing style, and historical situations have so much in common. The name used today to designate them, "Pastoral Epistles," was first used in the eighteenth century because of the attention given in them to the ministerial offices. The irony is that the word "pastor" is not used in the letters, although they do devote considerable space to the qualifications and responsibilities of church leaders.

Authorship

The most important historical question in the study of the Pastoral Epistles is the determination of who wrote them. I look first at the data that have raised questions about the identity of the author, and then I explore theories that have sought to explain the data.

The Place of the Pastorals in Ancient Manuscripts

The Pastoral Epistles were not easily accepted into the developing canon of the NT. They are lacking, for example, in the canon of Marcion in the mid-second century. Their omission could mean that Marcion knew them and did not like them (Tertullian's opinion, *Against Marcion* 5.21), or it could mean that he did not know them, perhaps because they were not yet written. *The Gospel of Truth*, a Gnostic tractate that also appeared near A.D. 150, seems to quote every book of the NT—except for these three. To complicate matters even more, Tatian accepted Titus but not 1 and 2 Timothy.

On the one hand, the Pastorals are missing from the important papyrus of Paul, p[46] (ca. 200), which breaks off without including them. For some scholars, the omission is proof that the letters were not readily acknowledged as authoritative. Others are not so sure that the Pastorals were omitted. Would the missing leaves have been enough for 1 Timothy, 2 Timothy, Titus, and the one other missing Pauline letter, Philemon? Probably not, although the scribe who copied this manuscript had begun to compress his letters to fit more text onto each page. Or the scribe may simply have omitted Philemon and the Pastorals because they are the four letters of Paul addressed to individuals rather than to congregations.[2]

On the other hand, quotations of 1 and 2 Timothy have been identified in Pol. *Phil.* 4.1; 9.2 (ca. 135–150). Yet this piece of information is ambiguous, too, as the supposed quotations are from passages in the Pastorals in which the author uses common philosophical sayings that Polycarp could well have quoted independently of the Pastorals.

By the final quarter of the second century the Pastorals were without doubt considered authoritative and written by Paul in such sources as the Muratorian Canon (although in an appendix), Athenagoras, Irenaeus, Clement of Alexandria, and Tertullian. Still, that evidence is rather late.

Chronology Presupposed in the Letters

The historical situation presupposed in the Pastoral Epistles demands that they were written *after* Paul was imprisoned in Rome (Acts 28:16, 30-31), because the geographical places and the order of the itineraries mentioned cannot be brought into Paul's life before then, as we know it from his undisputed letters[3] and Acts. All scholars agree on that judgment.

Thus 1 Tim. 1:3, where Paul has left for Macedonia and Timothy is directed to remain in Ephesus, cannot be fitted into the other information we have about their lives (see Acts 19:22). The directions Paul gives in 2 Tim. 4:13, 20 presuppose that he had recently been in Asia Minor. That information, too, is hard to reconcile with Acts, since in Acts Paul spent two years imprisoned in Caesarea before beginning the voyage to Rome. Nor can Titus be placed any more easily in Paul's life. The letter is set in Crete, where Paul has recently left Titus. The only otherwise-known stop Paul made in Crete is in Acts 27, but it was a brief stop with no indication of missionary work. For that matter, in Titus Paul spends the next winter in Nicopolis (3:12), whereas in Acts the winter is spent in Malta (28:1-11).

If the chronology of the Pastorals is accurate, Paul was not killed in Rome the first time around but was released. He returned to the eastern Mediterranean for further missionary work, was arrested once more, taken to Rome, and imprisoned a second time, following which he was martyred. Before his rearrest Paul wrote 1 Timothy and Titus; during his second imprisonment in Rome (2 Tim. 1:8, 16-17) he penned 2 Timothy. Once more, this supposed chronology clashes with Acts. In Acts 20:24-25, 38 Paul has no expectation of a return to the churches of Asia Minor, which most probably means that the author of Acts has no knowledge of later missionary activity of Paul in the East. In addition, Paul's hope, when writing to Rome while still free, was to travel from Corinth to Jerusalem to Rome to Spain (Rom. 15:24-25, 28). Further missionary activity was to occur in the far western reaches of the Mediterranean basin, not in the eastern portions.

But is there evidence of a release from the first imprisonment? *1 Clem.* 5.7, written about A.D. 96, says of Paul, "reaching the limits of the West, he bore witness before rulers." This passage, written in Rome, could well refer to a trip to Spain (from Rome's perspective, "the West"), which would presume a release from the (first) Roman imprisonment (Holtz, Brox, Kümmel). But "the West" could instead refer to the city of Rome itself, where Paul indeed bore his witness before rulers (Hultgren). Moreover, *1 Clement* does not know about a release. Other evidence for a journey to Spain (Muratorian Canon, lines 38–39) and of release from the first Roman imprisonment (Eusebius *Ecclesiastical History* 2.22) is weak, as the statements do not appear to be based on independent information but on the NT itself. A key factor here is that the Pastorals themselves know of no release for Paul.

Other chronological questions remain. Why would Paul need to set forth basic church regulations when he had just seen Timothy, who was a trusted, close companion of many years? Similar questions can be raised about Titus. Again, it seems odd that Paul would only now, after some years, ask for his personal items, when he anticipates that his death is near (2 Tim. 4:6-8, 13, 18).

Addressees

In the undisputed letters and in Acts, Timothy was a longtime trusted companion of Paul. The son of a Jewish Christian mother and a pagan father (Acts 16:1), he worked regularly with Paul (Acts 16:3; 17:14-15; 18:5; 19:22, 20:4; 1 Thess. 1:1; 2 Cor. 1:1, 19; Phil. 1:1; Philem. 1; cf. 2 Thess. 1:1). Paul evaluated his work highly (Phil. 2:19-24), with the result that Timothy was dispatched on special trips (1 Thess. 3:1-9; 1 Cor. 4:17, 16:10; Phil. 2:19, 23). Paul called Timothy his "beloved and faithful child in the Lord" (1 Cor. 4:17), "co-worker" (Rom. 16:21), and "our brother" (1 Thess. 3:2).

In the Pastorals the same intimacy is indicated in the phrases "loyal child" (1 Tim. 1:2; more literally, "legitimate child"; the phrase legitimates Timothy's role and the tradition he is to protect) and "beloved child" (2 Tim. 1:2; "my child" in 2:1). The Timothy of the Pastorals is not the strong figure of the undisputed letters, however. He is a hesitant, anxious, fearful young man who needs a good deal of encouragement to exercise his authority (1 Tim. 4:12; 5:23; 2 Tim. 1:8; 2:1). Still, he is to follow Paul as an interpreter of Scripture and guardian of the tradition (1 Tim.

6:20; 2 Tim. 1:11-14), and he has the special role of being a "man of God" (1 Tim. 6:11).

Titus was a Gentile Christian who accompanied Paul in Gal. 2:1, 3 to the so-called Apostolic Council. At that meeting the uncircumcised Titus was Paul's "audiovisual" argument that Gentiles did not need to be circumcised in order to be Christians. He played a prominent mediatorial role in the events underlying 2 Corinthians (2:13; 7:6-7, 13-15; 8:6, 16-23; 12:18). In the Pastorals, he too is called a "loyal child" (Titus 1:4), who needs to be reminded of his authority and encouraged to use it (2:1-8). Instructions in this letter seem also to be more elementary than would be expected for a veteran, successful missionary (1:5).

For some scholars the discrepancies between the views of Timothy and Titus in the undisputed letters and in the Pastorals constitute a datum that is inconsistent with authorship by Paul. To such scholars, Timothy and Titus are paradigmatic, not historical, figures who provide the necessary chronological and authoritative links between Paul's time and the time of the writing of the letters (D. MacDonald, Quinn, Fiore).

View of Paul

The Pastoral Epistles portray Paul as the quintessential sinner, as *the* apostle, and as the prototypical martyr.

First, Paul is a sinner. Part of his gratitude to God is the realization that God had chosen him "even though I was formerly a blasphemer, a persecutor, and a man of violence" (1 Tim. 1:13). Jesus came into the world to save sinners—of whom Paul is the "foremost" (1 Tim. 1:15-16; cf. 1 Cor. 15:9; Eph. 3:8).

Second, Paul is pictured not only as *an* apostle (1 Tim. 2:7; 2 Tim. 1:11) but in fact as *the* apostle (indeed, he is the only one named). No longer must he fight for recognition of his authority, as in the undisputed letters. Paul is therefore *the* authority figure of the documents and is the guarantor and interpreter of the tradition (1 Tim. 4:1-16).

He is, finally, the prototype of the martyr (2 Tim. 1:11-12; 2:8-10; 3:10-11; 4:6-8). His suffering, based on that of Jesus (2 Tim. 4:16), provides a model for other Christians who will have to testify (2 Tim. 4:17). The author may even see the suffering of Paul as in some way of vicarious significance for others (2 Tim. 2:10; cf. Eph. 3:13 and Col. 1:24). The theology of suffering extends beyond Paul to Timothy (1 Tim. 1:18-19a; 4:10; 6:12; 2 Tim. 1:8; 2:3; 3:10-17; 4:5) and, through Timothy, to all church leaders. Suffering is ultimately the lot of all Christians (2 Tim. 3:12).

For many commentators the threefold emphasis on Paul goes beyond what the historical Paul wrote. In particular, the focus on Paul as the sole apostle and as the source of a piety of suffering may indicate a backward glance possible only after his martyrdom.

Vocabulary and Style

Although all NT documents contain words not found elsewhere in the NT, the use of such words in the Pastorals is at a rate two and a half times that of the undisputed letters,[4] a rate by far the highest of the Pauline letters (Harrison). Grayston and Herdan have used more sophisticated linguistic theories to update Harrison. When Hultgren compares the vocabulary of the Pastorals with the other ten letters attributed to Paul, he counts 306 words (or 36 percent of the vocabulary) as unique to the Pastorals. In addition, over one-third of those words (or 14 percent of the overall vocabulary of the Pastorals) does not appear until writings of the second century, a factor that "pulls" the Pastorals toward a later date of composition.

The issue of vocabulary and style is also a matter of content.

1. Important Pauline words and phrases are missing in the Pastorals: righteousness of God, cross, freedom, body of Christ (*sōma*, "body," does not occur at all), proclaim the gospel, boast, wisdom, soul/life (*psychē*), and revelation. The contrast in Paul between flesh and spirit is also missing.

2. Words that have one meaning in the undisputed letters often have a different meaning in the Pastorals. The primary example is the word "faith." Although it can mean obedient trust (as in Paul), it is normatively used in the Pastorals to designate (a) "the Christian faith" as a distinct religion, with emphasis on its teachings (1 Tim. 1:2; 3:9, 13; 4:1, 6; 5:8; 6:10, 12, 21; 2 Tim. 2:18; 4:7; Titus 1:4, 13; 3:15) or (b) faith as a Christian virtue (1 Tim. 1:5, 14, 19; 4:12; 6:11; 2 Tim. 2:22; 3:10; Titus 2:2, 10).

Nor is "faith" the only such word. "In Christ" is used in the Pastorals with abstract nouns in a nonpersonal way (e.g., 1 Tim. 1:14; 3:13; 2 Tim. 1:1; 2:10). In the undisputed letters it refers to a deeply personal relationship between the believer and Christ. Nor does the term *dikaiosynē* refer to justification in the way it is found, for example, in Rom. 3:21-28. In the Pastorals the term refers to being upright or moral (1 Tim. 6:11; 2 Tim. 2:22; 3:16; 4:8). Law is no longer the issue it was in the undisputed letters, and the sole discussion understands the function of the law to be the opposite of what Paul outlined (1 Tim. 1:8-9).[5]

3. Words used in the undisputed letters are replaced with other words. Paul uses the word *eucharistein* ("I give thanks"), but in 1 Tim. 1:12 and 2 Tim. 1:3 a different phrase is used (*charis echein*, "I have grace/thanks"). Paul uses "lord" (*kyrios*) for the owner of slaves (Rom. 14:4; Gal. 4:1; e.g.), whereas the Pastorals have "master" (*despotēs* 1 Tim. 6:1-2; Titus 2:9; cf. 2 Tim. 2:21).

4. The words and phrases found in the Pastorals but nowhere else in Paul are frequent and theologically significant. "The saying is sure" (1 Tim. 1:15; 3:1; 4:9; 2 Tim. 2:11; Titus 3:8); "a good conscience" (1 Tim. 1:5, 19) and "clear conscience" (1 Tim. 3:9; 2 Tim. 1:3); "godliness" or "religion" (*eusebeia*; 1 Tim. 2:2; 3:16; 4:7-8; 6:3, 5, 6, 11; 2 Tim. 3:5; Titus 1:1); "decently/modesty" (*sōphrosynē*; 1 Tim. 2:9, 15); and "reverence for God" (1 Tim. 2:10) are all absent from the undisputed letters. The salvific event is also spoken of in language unusual for Paul (Titus 2:10-11, 13; 3:4), with many of the terms ("appear," "training," "loving kindness," "Savior," "manifestation") representing an adoption of Hellenistic terminology that exceeds that of Paul himself.

5. The distinctions in vocabulary extend also to short, seemingly insignificant terms. Many short words frequently used in the undisputed letters are missing in the Pastorals: "therefore" (*dio*), "yet" (*eti*), "so that" (*hōste*), "ever" (*an*), "whether" (*eite*), "each" (*hekastos*), "now" (*nyni*), "no longer" (*ouketi*), "again" (*palin*), "with" (*syn*), and "just as" (*hōsper*). Harrison argues that it is often in such short words that the style of an author comes through in its most characteristic form—and in a form most difficult to reproduce. Two statistics must suffice: In the undisputed letters "so that" (*hōste*) occurs thirty-seven times but not at all in the Pastorals. Paul uses the word "with" (*syn*) twenty-eight times in the undisputed letters, often with great theological weight. It too never occurs in the Pastorals.

6. In writing style, the Pastorals are much closer to Hellenistic literature of the day and further away from the style of the Septuagint than the undisputed letters of Paul. Beyer computes that the Pastorals have ten to twenty times as many "Grecisms" as the other Pauline letters.[6]

For most scholars these data can adequately be explained only by the conclusion that Paul is not the author. Others doubt the value of any statistical work or think that the data base is too small.[7] Perhaps Paul changed his approach during the years since his last surviving letter, or perhaps he was speaking to a more thoroughly hellenized audience, or perhaps he utilized specialized language in writing against his Gnostically influenced opponents. Perhaps Paul is more influenced at this point in his life by Latinisms, given his Roman imprisonment (Spicq). Yet the sheer amount and the quality of the data from differences in vocabulary and style remain. The question is whether the counterarguments are able to overcome those differences.

Use of Other Pauline Letters

The author of the Pastorals exhibits knowledge of other Pauline letters. Hanson identifies twenty-one "clear echoes" of Paul.[8] The chief parallels cited are 1 Tim. 6:12/Phil. 3:12-14; 2 Tim. 1:6-9/Rom. 8:12-17; 2 Tim. 3:16-17/Rom. 15:4-6; and 2 Tim. 4:6-8/Phil. 2:16-17. In each case the author of the Pastorals has apparently reapplied to his own situation material from the undisputed letters. The implications of this phenomenon are debatable. For example, Hanson and Roloff argue that the use of the undisputed letters is a sign of the lateness and non-Pauline authorship of the Pastorals. Others could respond: "Of course the author uses material from the earlier letters. He wrote them!"

Method of Handling Heresy

Greater unanimity appears in scholarly discussions regarding the way in which the author deals with heresy.[9] Timothy is directed to order[10] people to stop teaching different doctrine (1 Tim. 1:3). False teachers and their speculations are to be avoided (2 Tim. 2:14, 16; 1 Tim. 4:7; 6:20). Such persons are, in fact, to be silenced (Titus 1:11). Relatively little is said, however, about the opponents themselves, other than the need to combat them (e.g., 1 Tim. 1:6-7), and much of what *is* said is theological name-calling, as Karris has shown. Yet the author is concerned about the opponents: rebuking them has as its goal "that they may become sound in the faith" (Titus 1:13).

In the undisputed letters Paul argues his case by utilizing his opponents' language and themes. In the Pastorals heresy is combated by means of tradition. The author does not argue with the heretics (with the possible exception of 1 Tim. 4:1-5), for they do not agree with the tradition (1 Tim. 6:20; cf. 2 Tim. 1:14; 2:2).

Church Organization

The terms "elder" (*presbyteros*) and "bishop" (*episkopos*), which are so important in the Pastorals, are used differently from their use in the undisputed letters. The first term is absent from the undisputed letters. "Bishop" occurs only one time in the undisputed letters, where it is in the plural (Phil. 1:1). In the Pastorals it is found only in the singular (1 Tim. 3:2, Titus 1:7). Moreover, the ordering of the church found in the Pastorals—bishop, elder, and deacon—is not evident in the undisputed letters. The issue is not only a matter of titles and rank, though. The various offices and their occupants assume a centrality not seen in the undisputed letters. Käsemann in particular has identified in the Pastorals a narrowing of the concept of *charisma* ("spiritual gift"). In 1 Tim. 4:14 and 2 Tim. 1:6, the word *charisma* is used only for an officeholder, whereas in the undisputed letters the Spirit gives *charisma* to every believer at baptism (Rom. 12:3-8; 1 Cor. 12:4-11). For many commentators the church in the Pastorals has reached a stage of organizational development beyond that of the undisputed letters.

Theology

Understanding of Christ and God.   Much of the Christology in the Pastorals is different from that of the undisputed letters. The Jesus of the parousia is unabashedly called God (Titus 2:13). The author also prays to Jesus as God (assuming that "Lord" means Jesus in 2 Tim. 4:18). But Jesus is never called "son of God" nor is the cross specifically mentioned. What does appear with some frequency is the word "epiphany" (*epiphaneia*; NRSV "appearing" or "manifestation") and the related verb. The terms, which are not used in the undisputed letters, refer in the Pastorals both to the first appearance of Jesus (2 Tim. 1:10; Titus 2:11; 3:4) and to his return (1 Tim. 6:14; 2 Tim. 4:1, 8; Titus 2:13). There is, therefore, an "epiphany Christology" in these letters, with God's saving activity in Jesus bracketed by two epiphanies with an "in-between time" stretching from the first epiphany to the second.

Apart from Christ, the major titles the author uses for Jesus are *kyrios* ("lord") and *sōtēr* ("savior"). *Kyrios* is the normative title given in Paul's letters to Jesus. *Sōtēr*, however, occurs only one time in the undisputed letters, in Phil. 3:20, where it has an eschatological reference. Whereas in the undisputed letters *kyrios* is normatively used for Jesus and the one use of *sōtēr* is definitely reserved for Jesus, in the Pastorals the titles are used interchangeably for God and Christ. The increased use of "savior" is another indication of greater use of Hellenistic terminology, since "savior" is used for the Roman emperor as well as for mystery religion deities; "epiphany" is another term from Hellenistic cults, often used for the appearance of a god, especially during processions.[11] Jesus is also called "mediator" (1 Tim. 2:5), a term used in Paul for Moses (Gal. 3:19-20).

There are certainly points of continuity. "Christ" is the most common title given to Jesus. God's grace is revealed through Jesus (2 Tim. 1:9-10). Justification is by grace (Titus 3:7), through faith alone, not works (2 Tim. 1:9; 3:15; Titus 3:5). The saying that Christ "gave himself a ransom for all" (1 Tim. 2:6) contains the Pauline theme of Jesus' self-giving for others (Gal. 1:4, 2:20; 2 Cor. 5:15; also Eph. 5:2, 25; and Titus 2:14).

As already indicated, God is also designated as "Savior" (1 Tim. 1:1; 2:3; 4:10; Titus 1:3; 2:10; 3:4), which may be the letters' most important term for God. God "is the Savior of all people, especially of those who believe" (1 Tim. 4:10), and "God our Savior . . . desires everyone to be saved and to come to the knowledge of the truth" (1 Tim. 2:3-4; see also 2 Tim. 1:9; 4:18; Titus 3:5). God's saving will is directed to all people, perhaps in contrast to the conception among some Gnostics that only certain people are eligible to be saved. Because of God's saving will, "Christ Jesus came into the world to save sinners" (1 Tim. 1:15). God is also called "blessed," a term used in nonbiblical Greek for the condition of the gods. In the NT it is used for God only in 1 Tim. 1:11 and 6:15. Other designations of God that are unique to the Pastorals include "King of the ages" (1 Tim. 1:17), "the blessed and only Sovereign" (6:15), and "he alone who has immortality and dwells in unapproachable light" (6:16).

Christian Life as Piety.   An important theme is the understanding of Christian life as "piety" or "godliness" (*eusebeia*; 1 Tim. 2:2; 3:16; 4:7-8; 6:3, 5-6, 11; 2 Tim. 3:5; Titus 1:1; the adverb is used in 2 Tim. 3:12 and Titus 2:12, and the verb in 1 Tim. 5:4).[12] The term is not found in any other Pauline letter. *Eusebeia* was what a person owed to God, to other persons, and to self. Hellenistic Jews used the term to explain their religion to the non-Jewish Greek-speaking world; thus it became a bridge term to that world. The comparable Latin term was *pietas*, which referred to the basic devotion of the Roman populace to the cults and gods that were believed to ensure the well-being of the Roman state. It is thus quite natural that *eusebeia* should occur in a context dealing with prayer for the rulers. What is somewhat unusual is the desire for Christians to "lead a quiet and peaceable life in all godliness and dignity" (1 Tim. 2:2; see also Titus 2:12). The undisputed letters have an eschatological tension: this world is passing away; the true home for Christians is above, and Christians therefore are in but not of the world. The Pastorals seem to suggest that Christians are in the world and of the world, but as Christians. At the same time, the author is aware that living piously can put the believer into conflict with society (2 Tim. 3:12).

Eschatology.   The normative scholarly view has sharply separated the eschatology of the Pastorals from that of the undisputed letters. The Pastorals are viewed as giving up the imminent expectation of the end and focusing instead on the present, with the church as institution at the center. The future hope of the return of Jesus is more a theological datum than a living expectation.

Nonetheless, the Pastorals combine a realized eschatology with an eschatological reservation. Salvation has already been given (2 Tim. 1:9-10; Titus 3:5). The believer can also "take hold of" eternal life in the present (1 Tim. 6:12, 19). Yet there is a futurity to salvation, as already seen in the discussion of "epiphany" (see also 1 Tim. 4:16; 2 Tim. 2:10-11; 4:18; Titus 1:2, 2:13; 3:7). It is the opponents who in particular stress that the resurrection has already occurred (2 Tim. 2:18); it is likely that the author of the Pastorals emphasizes futurity in opposition to them.

The question still to be answered is how imminent is the expectation of the end. Quinn and Kidd point to predictions of end-time heresies that are being fulfilled as proof of an imminent expectation. What they fail to account for is the use by our author of traditional material.[13] The presence of similar material in 2 Thess. 2:3, 11-12 and 2 Pet. 2:1-3; 3:3-4—in documents that clearly put off the end of time into the far-distant future— illustrates that sheer usage of such motifs does not necessarily signal imminent expectation. The Pastorals have nothing comparable to Rom. 13:11-14 and 1 Thess. 4:13—5:11. Nor have proponents of an apocalyptic eschatology in the Pastorals explained how tradition and office, which enable the church to settle in for an indefinite future, are to be reconciled with a supposed imminent expectation. Further, the radical break identified by Paul between the old age and the new age is not evident in these letters (Titus 2:12 and 1 Tim. 6:17; but contrast 2 Tim. 4:10). Thus in the matter of eschatology the Pastorals once more are on a different theological track from that of the undisputed letters.

Miscellaneous Theological Positions. Tradition is viewed as a guarantor of the faith. Offices need to be established in order to protect the tradition and hand it on inviolate (2 Tim. 2:2). The result is emphasis on "sound" or "healthy teaching" (1 Tim. 1:10; 4:6; 2 Tim. 4:3; Titus 1:9; 2:1; other references to teaching are 1 Tim. 4:13, 16; 5:17; 6:1, 3; 2 Tim. 3:10, 16; Titus 2:7, 10). Another resulting emphasis is the importance of knowledge of the truth, with "truth" referring to correct belief in Christ (1 Tim. 2:4; 4:3; 2 Tim. 2:25; 3:7; Titus 1:1). The church is thus understood as "the pillar and bulwark of the truth" (1 Tim. 3:15).

The undisputed letters are quite concerned about the positive ethical outcome of faith. "Works," when not an attempt at self-justification, are the fruit of the Spirit (e.g., Gal. 5:22-26). In the Pastorals "good works" are more prominently displayed and more strongly emphasize human initiative (1 Tim. 2:10; 5:10, 25; 6:18; 2 Tim. 2:21; 3:17; Titus 2:7, 14; 3:1, 8, 14). Moreover, the Spirit is much less significant in the Pastorals. Only twice is the indwelling Spirit mentioned (2 Tim. 1:14; Titus 3:5), and only once is it the eschatological gift (in material quoted in Titus 3:5).

Finally, the place of women is quite different from that of the undisputed letters (Gal. 3:28; Rom. 16:1-3, 6-7; 1 Cor. 7:1-7; even 11:2-16). The more egalitarian view of the undisputed letters is replaced by an attempt to reassign women to their traditional roles (1 Tim. 2:8-15; 5:3-16).

The theological differences between the Pastorals and the undisputed letters are substantial, so substantial that for a host of commentators the distinctions in theology are determinative.

Explanations of the Data: Authorship Theories

Paul as Author. The traditional position is that the author is who the letters say he is: Paul (Spicq, Guthrie, Kelly, and Johnson). In addition to denial of the arguments advanced above and suggestions of time gap, changed situation, or advancing age, Kelly and Guthrie maintain that the letters go back to Paul because they read like real letters. Both rely on the "feel" of the letters, with the underlying assumption being that the letters could have this "feel" only if they go back to Paul. Johnson accounts for the differences in language by arguing that the Pastorals have "discussion of matters inappropriate for letters written for community consumption."[14]

A Secretary as Author. Other scholars have developed a mediating position: Paul gave the general outline of the letters but left the actual wording to his secretary.[15] Roller, Jeremias, Spicq, Moule, and Kelly have all adopted this thesis in one form or another. For Roller and Jeremias, Paul handed the secretary notes that the secretary edited into complete letters, which Paul then corrected and signed. The use of a secretary accounts, therefore, for the differences between the Pastorals and the undisputed letters. In contrast, Kelly sees the secretary as in constant contact with Paul, which accounts for the elements more consonant with the undisputed letters. Thus Kelly has Paul as the source of the letter, but the secretary has so much freedom that the wording is really his. The work is Paul's but not Paul's!

One might well ask in what meaningful way Paul remains the author. The argument that such a process was necessary because of Paul's imprisonment has validity only for 2 Timothy, since neither of the other two is a prison epistle. At the same time, the uniformity of language among the three letters points to the same author. The secretary theory raises as many problems as it initially appears to solve and, ironically, points to someone other than Paul as the author.

Luke as Author. Moule, Wilson, and Quinn, among others, propose that Luke wrote or compiled the Pastorals. Moule's position is actually a combination of the secretary and the Lukan hypotheses: Luke wrote the letters during Paul's lifetime, at Paul's request, but only in part at Paul's dictation. Moule has Luke write the Pastorals first, then Acts. Wilson reverses the order, with Luke utilizing Paul's travel notes and several letters. Quinn maintains that the author of Luke-Acts wrote the Pastorals as an epistolary appendix to the larger work. The proponents of this position point to similarities in the view of Paul, eschatology, social ethics, interest in good order, and the law, as well as vocabulary.[16] An oft-cited example is Acts 20:18-35/2 Tim. 4:6-8.

To others the commonalities are too general to sustain common authorship but are typical of gentile, Hellenistic Christianity of the third generation. Further, the differences between Luke-Acts and the Pastorals are substantial. The Pastorals have no salvation-historical perspective; Luke-Acts has nothing similar to epiphany Christology. Conversely, the Lukan "Son of God" and the consistent role for the Spirit are missing from the Pastorals. The key is the hesitancy in Acts to give Paul the title of apostle. In Acts he is subordinate to the Jerusalem Twelve. In the Pastorals he is independent of Jerusalem and functions as *the* apostle. Further, Acts does not mention Titus and has nothing about Timothy as Paul's representative in Ephesus. Even Moule admits the serious objection that the Pastorals lack the sort of short words from Luke important to authorship theories.[17] Finally, Luke is concerned to connect the message about Jesus with the OT, but such a concern is hardly evident in the Pastorals.

Fragment Hypothesis.   Scholars have long proposed variations of a fragment theory: the bulk of the Pastorals is pseudonymous but embedded in them are fragments that go back to Paul. The key to their identification is their personal nature. The list of fragments varies, but most who work with this theory list 2 Tim. 4:9-21 (perhaps without v. 18) and Titus 3:12-15; 2 Tim. 1:15-18 and 1 Tim. 1:20; 5:23 also are frequently considered to be fragments of genuine Paul material. Fuller posited a descending scale for the use of such fragments: 2 Timothy, written first, is possibly structured around a genuine farewell letter from Paul; Titus, written next, has few or no such historical sections; 1 Timothy has no personal notes at all, for now the author is confident enough to stand on his own feet—or he has run out of genuine materials. The fragment theories accomplish two objectives: they "solve," for some advocates of pseudonymous authorship, the presence of highly personal material that seems as though it should go back to Paul; and they connect the Pastorals with the historical Paul himself.

The difficulties with these theories are substantial. There is no exact parallel in ancient literature to such a procedure. If the fragments are parts of larger documents, what has happened to those documents? For Hanson, earlier an advocate of a fragment hypothesis, the key question is whether these fragments could have survived only as fragments, for certainly one cannot structure from them a full letter. The variation in the identification of the fragments also illustrates that the distinctions between the language and content of the supposed fragments and the rest of the letters are not self-evident.

A final question is the function of these passages. Those who argue for the use of the fragments by a pseudonymous author contend that he used them to lend credibility to his letters. The materials also have an additional literary function: the motif of items left behind (2 Tim. 4:13), for example, is frequent in pseudepigraphic literature as well as in papyrus letters written by poor people and may well be part of the idealization of Paul, who has only one cloak and who needs, in addition, only the parchments to carry out his work (cf. 1 Tim. 6:8). Paul is the model of the poor Christian missionary.[18] On balance, it seems probable that the fragments that have been identified do not predate the Pastorals themselves but come from the hand of the author.

Pseudonymous Author.   The weight of the evidence outlined leads to the conclusion that an unknown Christian, writing in Paul's name, produced the letters. Pseudonymous writing was not considered illegitimate or improper in the ancient world. Indeed, it was considered the sincerest form of flattery and was understood to be a way to keep current the influence of an important figure (e.g., Tertullian *Against Marcion* 4.5). The writing of pseudonymous letters was common both in Judaism and in Christianity (Epistle of Jeremiah, *Epistle of Aristeas*, 1 and 2 Peter, Jude, James, Revelation, Acts 23:26-30, *2 Clement, Barnabas*). The Pythagoreans also passed on the teachings of their master in a large number of works that were written as though they were from the historical Pythagoras—even though it was widely known that he did not write anything. There are also writings associated with the name of Plato, especially letters, that came from followers who lived centuries after his death. Indeed, a normal exercise in ancient schools was for the student to write a speech or letter as the speech or letter would have been composed by a famous person or mythical figure.[19]

It is highly probable that the author of the Pastorals understood himself to be in continuity with Paul and able to express what Paul would have said had he still been alive. Indeed, Donelson concludes that "the Pastorals conform beautifully to the pseudepigraphical letter genre."[20]

Situation Presupposed in the Letters

Social Setting

The church of the Pastorals is organized with the Greco-Roman household as the model (the church is "the household of God," 1 Tim. 3:15). Within that structure are clear distinctions between men and women, masters and slaves, wealthy and poor, parents and children, and socially superior and socially inferior in a complex set of relationships.

Frequent references to wealth and to wealthy people indicate that some in the community were relatively well-to-do, including women who could afford expensive clothes (1 Tim. 2:9; the contrast between fancy dress and modest behavior is a common topic in philosophical literature of the time). There were certainly poor widows in the congregation, but 1 Tim. 5:16 shows that there were enough wealthier women that the author could expect them to be the benefactors of the poor widows.

Likewise there are indications that the bishop was to be well situated financially, at least relative to other members of the congregation. "Whoever aspires to the office of bishop desires a noble task" (1 Tim. 3:1) uses the language employed for wealthier citizens who "aspired" to the "noble task" of municipal office.[21] Further, the bishop is to be hospitable (1 Tim. 3:2; Titus 1:8), which may well presume the financial capability to be hospitable. It is also quite possible that persons who were able to host the congregation in their homes often became the leaders.[22] In addition, the passages dealing with slaves and masters (1 Tim. 6:1-2; Titus 2:9-10) evidence an attitude that is more in tune with attitudes of slave owners than with attitudes of slaves. The comments about "those who want to be rich" and the love of money (1 Tim. 6:9-10), as well as the directives to those who are rich (1 Tim. 6:17-19), also point toward congregational members who had some financial means.

All of that material, however, should not lead to the conclusion that the congregation(s) of the Pastorals were composed of upper-class people. The congregations founded by Paul and his associates probably had no members of the upper classes, nor did they likely have many from the lowest groups on the societal scale. Rather the congregations were composed of people who worked with their hands (artisans), shopkeepers, and at least some well-situated people of relative means, together with extended families (including slaves).[23]

Disputes Within the Church

Dispute over Proper Teachings. In 1 Timothy Paul's lieutenant is to "instruct certain people not to teach any different doctrine, and not to occupy themselves with myths and endless genealogies that promote speculations" (1:3-7; on myths see 4:7; 2 Tim. 4:4; Titus 1:14). Since Timothy is directed to instruct them, it is safe to assume that these opponents are members of the congregation. Certainly those who "have suffered shipwreck in the faith" are or have been members (1 Tim. 1:19-20). It is quite possible that among the leaders in the group opposed by the author are women, which might in part explain his refusal to have women teaching or in authority over a man (2:12). It is also possible that the emphasis on childbirth may be constructed to oppose a negative view of creation (2:15). For that matter, the opponents forbid marriage (4:3). They also demand abstinence from some foods, to which the author responds by pointing to the goodness of God's creation (4:3-5). Related may be the counsel in 5:23 that Timothy "take a little wine" and "no longer drink only water." In relationship to the author, the opponents teach "otherwise" (*heteros*, in a heretical way; 1:3; 6:3) and are prey to various moral failings (6:3-5), including being charlatans (6:5). From the author's perspective the opponents engage in "the profane chatter and contradictions of what is falsely called knowledge" (6:20).

In 2 Timothy, Timothy is to warn the opponents "that they are to avoid wrangling over words" (2:14, 23). The talk of the opponents—as opposed to Paul's healthy teaching and the directive rightly to explain the word of truth (2:15)—spreads like gangrene, putrifying and killing as it goes (2:17). They claim that the resurrection has already occurred (2:18).[24] The possibility of repentance is mentioned (2:21), and therefore the Lord's servant must be "patient, correcting opponents with gentleness" (2:24-25). Why? "God may perhaps grant that they will repent and come to know the truth" (2:25). In 3:1-5 the author applies a standard list of vices to his opponents: essentially they are outwardly religious but inwardly empty. Here, too, the opponents are connected with women in the congregation (3:6-7).

Titus applies much of the same language to the opponents, referring also to "those of the circumcision" (1:10). In Titus "they must be silenced, since they are upsetting whole families by teaching for sordid gain what it is not right to teach" (1:11). The sharpness of the response to the opponents still has the goal of restoration (1:13), which will include leaving behind Jewish myths, human commandments, and purity laws (1:14-15). Until that happens "they are detestable, disobedient, unfit for any good work" (1:16).

As Karris has shown, much of the language used against the opponents is typical of the polemic that philosophers used against the Sophists. When that language has been identified, a core of reliable information about the opponents remains. The references to the law and to Jewish myths point toward a Jewish Christian group or a group enamored of Judaism. At the same time the emphasis on knowledge, speculations, genealogies, various asceticisms, and the view that the resurrection has already occurred sound Gnostic.[25] The opponents seek to combine into one religion Pauline Christianity, more specifically Jewish Christian thought, and emerging Gnostic positions.[26]

Dispute over the Proper Role for Women.   First Tim. 2:8-15 contains an extensive section on the role of women that may have been, as we have seen, in part written to respond to the opponents. 2 Timothy speaks of "silly women, overwhelmed by their sins and swayed by all kinds of desires" (3:6). Titus 2:3-5 directs older women to be reverent, not slanderers, and not given to drink. Widows in particular present a problem for the author. The question of how to determine truly needy widows is a difficult one (1 Tim. 5:3-16), which is complicated by younger widows who, from the author's perspective, have become idle and gad about from house to house as gossips and busybodies (5:11-13).

Two factors that may have influenced the women of the Pastorals (and thereby the author) are the cult of the goddess Artemis and the *Acts of Paul and Thecla*. Gritz places 1 Timothy in Ephesus, where the cult of the Mother Goddess was popular and influential. Through the teachers, the beliefs and practices of that cult, including relative freedom for women and the seductive dress often adopted by devotees of Artemis, had infiltrated the congregation's female members. D. MacDonald has turned in a different direction, to the *Acts of Paul and Thecla*, which were written in Asia Minor between A.D. 150 and 190. They tell the story of Paul and a female convert of his, Thecla. The material is clearly legendary, but it is also, MacDonald has argued, based on oral traditions that were handed on from the first into the second century. The Paul of these *Acts* is a radical feminist who counsels women to leave their families and follow the celibate life, independent of their dominating husbands and their children (cf. 2 Tim. 3:6-7). These stories about Paul circulate, according to MacDonald's thesis, among women (thus the old wives' tales, 1 Tim. 4:7) and are spread as women go from house to house (1 Tim. 5:13). MacDonald understands the Pastorals as written in opposition to the oral legends that form the heart of the *Acts*.

Relationship to Society

The dispute over the role of women leads one to consider the relationship of the church(es) of the Pastorals with the surrounding society. The thesis of Wilken is that Roman society viewed early Christianity as an atheistic, impious superstition that corrupted households and thereby the entire society.[27] Celsus referred to the difficulties created in the household when Christianity was introduced (Origen *Contra Celsum* 3.55). In addition, in the ancient world there was the long-standing discussion on household management that maintained that the household was the basic building block of the whole society.[28] Anything that threatened that building block was therefore suspect. By creating a new social group that functioned independently of the rest of society, Christianity appeared to threaten the well-being of Rome.

In the Pastorals one has a constant sense that the "world" is looking over the shoulder of the author. In other documents of the early church, such as Revelation, the author does not care what the society thinks. In these letters, however, the author cares very much, which we see reflected in his use of household codes, leadership virtues, and descriptions of the role of women, all of which he adopted from the society and all of which counter the positions of his opponents. It may well be that part of his fear of the opponents is the potential that their views have of drawing inappropriate attention from the surrounding Greco-Roman society.

Date and Place

Where and when one places the writing of these letters depends on decisions about authorship, since the letters have no clear references to external historical events. If Paul wrote them, they had to have been written near the end of his life (the early 60s) and from a place of imprisonment (traditionally assigned to Rome).

If Paul is not the author, other possibilities exist. Bauer and von Campenhausen have argued that the letters were written against the Gnostic heretic Marcion, specifically against his document entitled "Antitheses."[29] The key evidence is that the term *antitheses* appears in 1 Tim. 6:20. If written against Marcion, the Pastorals could not have been written before 150. The heresy combated in these letters is not similar enough to his thought to sustain the thesis, however. The heresy fought in the Pastorals is a Jewish Gnosticism, with makes positive use of the OT (1 Tim. 1:7; Titus 1:14), whereas Marcion was anti-Jewish. In addition, no argument in the Pastorals is against specific views of Marcion. A variation of the Marcion thesis is von Campenhausen's position that Polycarp penned these letters in opposition to Marcion. In addition to the improbability of a Marcion connection, the language and style of Polycarp's letters are less literary than the Pastorals, and Polycarp's understanding of faith is much closer to Paul than to the Pastorals. Easton also showed in detail the likelihood that Polycarp used the Pastorals in composing his letter to the Philippians.

The developing church structure, which has not yet reached the stage of *1 Clement*, Ignatius of Antioch, or Polycarp; the incipient Jewish Gnosticism opposed; the sense that the Pauline tradition is still very much alive; and the presupposition of a collection but not yet a set canon of Paul's letters—all point to a date of origin that is relatively early. Given the dating of Ignatius between 107 and 117 and his reference to the fact that the Ephesian church had stabilized and rebuffed wicked teaching (Ign. *Eph.* 4.1; 9.1) and the argument that Ephesus is the likely site of writing (see below), and given the probability that Polycarp used the Pastorals, one arrives at an upper date of the early second century. If the Pastorals do know Acts, the letters could not have been written before 85 or 90. Thus a date in the 90s or early 100s is probable. Such a date fits the implicit time frame of the letters: the first generation (Paul) is writing to the second generation (Timothy and Titus) to set up structures for the third generation (the church[es] of the Pastorals). A date in the 90s or early 100s also explains the vocabulary from the Pastorals that is otherwise attested only in those decades.[30]

Somewhat more data exist for determining the locale of the recipients. That the word "bishop" occurs only in the singular in the Pastorals provides a link to Asia Minor, where monepiscopacy first developed. In addition, much of Asia Minor had been Pauline mission territory, and the Pastorals are clearly written to a group that reveres Paul. Recent thought has centered on Ephesus (1 Tim. 1:3; 2 Tim. 1:18; 4:12) as both the destination of the letters (at least 1 and 2 Timothy) and the source. Hultgren has shown that eighteen of the twenty-eight persons named in the Pastorals (leaving out OT names, Jesus, and Pontius Pilate) have documented connections with Ephesus; three more were known to believers in Ephesus. The probable existence in Ephesus of a Pauline school makes Ephesus an even more likely site. The Ephesian connection for Titus is more tenuous, but it is quite possible that work on Crete was part of missionary activity originating in Ephesus.

The major competitor is Rome. In the fictive situation of 2 Timothy Paul is probably in that city (1:8, 16-17; 4:16). Quinn thinks it possible that the author wrote the letters to rehabilitate Paul, who had been martyred in Rome. For Quinn the Pastorals reflect the original Jewish Christian organization of the church in Rome. At the same time he proposes that, just as Timothy and Titus are representative figures, so too are the congregations: Crete stands for newer Jewish Christian congregations, Ephesus for the racially mixed congregations in the great cities of Asia Minor.

On balance, the specific evidence for Ephesus as the home of the Pastorals seems stronger than that for Rome.

Purpose

The basic purpose for the writing of these letters is contained in 1 Tim. 3:14-15: "I hope to come to you soon, but I am writing these instructions to you so that, if I am delayed, you may know how one ought to behave in the household of God, which is the church of the living God, the pillar and bulwark of the truth." The letters are written, therefore, for the following reasons:

1. To reaffirm the connection and continuity between the historical Paul and the recipients of the letters, thus reasserting the Pauline tradition;

2. To state what Paul would have said against the heretics, had he been alive at the time of the writing of the letters;

3. To outline how these congregations are to carry out their mission to sinners (1 Tim. 1:15) so that all might be saved and come to the knowledge of the truth (1 Tim. 2:4);

4. To detail "how one ought to behave" in carrying out the mission;

5. To state the proper relationship of the Christian to society;

6. To develop further what the author considered good order, particularly in relationship to church offices, women, and the opponents. A specific problem for the author is the relationship of social superiors and social inferiors, a problem that underlies purposes 4, 5, and 6;

7. To prepare Christians for an indefinitely long future.

Rhetorical Structure

The genre of the three documents is that of letters. A more precise rhetorical category for 1 Timothy and Titus is parenesis, a type of ethical exhortation. 2 Timothy is also parenetic, although the more specific genre is the literary testament or farewell, in which the dying figure addresses his or her descendants (here, the "beloved child" Timothy, 1:2, and through him other church leaders). In 2 Timothy the parenesis has a special pathos, as the dying apostle (4:6-8) charges his successor to share in suffering (2:3-15).

Determination of the original order of the letters continues to baffle scholars. Hanson decides that Titus is last, as the author was running out of material! Easton places them in the order 2 Timothy (written ca. 95), Titus (100), 1 Timothy (105), based on the progression he identifies in the concern for church order, the progressive decrease in personal material, and changes in attitude toward the opponents. Fuller agrees. Among those who believe that Paul wrote the letters, 2 Timothy is often thought to be last in order, because of its nature as a last will and testament.

Quinn begins with the observation that the opening of Titus (1:1-4) is longer and more developed than the openings of the other letters. For him, the opening of Titus indicates that it once stood at the head of the collection of three letters and served as the prologue to the set. 1 Timothy builds on and further develops the introduction given in Titus to church offices, and 2 Timothy falls last because of its testamentary nature. In addition, 1 Timothy seems to end abruptly and yet flows right into 2 Timothy. Further, Quinn identifies in the order of the letters the classical Pauline theology of "to the Jew first" (Rom. 1:16), in that Titus is directed to predominantly Jewish Christian people. Quinn's position is supported by the Muratorian Canon and Ambrosiaster, which list the letters in the same order.

Beckwith supports the Titus, 1 Timothy, 2 Timothy order on rhetorical grounds. He works with the Pastorals as a unit and identifies them as an example of deliberative rhetoric that has been cast in the structure of three epistles. He outlines the three documents as a unified whole:

Proem:	Titus 1:1-3
Proposition:	Titus 1:5—3:14
Narration:	1 Tim. 1:3-17
Proof:	1 Tim. 1:18—6:21a
Refutation with Digression:	2 Tim. 1:8—2:26
Peroration:	2 Tim. 3:1—4:18

The theme, or the proposition of the proposition, would be Titus 2:11-14. Using Aristotle's categories of proof, Beckwith sees the three elements of *ethos*, *logos*, and *pathos* operating in the letters. Titus builds on the *ethos* of Paul as one who has the authority to direct the ministry of others. 1 Timothy uses logical argumentation, or *logos*. 2 Timothy, which contains most of the personal elements with particular attention on Paul's sufferings, exhibits the *pathos* that frequently closes such presentations, according to ancient rhetorical theorists.[31]

Why then do we have the canonical order of 1 Timothy, 2 Timothy, Titus? When the letters were added to the developing collection of Pauline Letters, they were appended as a unit—and in decreasing size. Such a pattern of organization was common in antiquity. That 1 Timothy is so much longer than the document immediately preceding it in the New Testament, 2 Thessalonians, probably indicates a division in the Pauline collection between the letters addressed to churches and those addressed to individuals. The objection that editors would not have changed the order of the three Pastoral Letters is removed when one remembers that the two-volume work of Luke-Acts was separated in the canon by the Gospel of John.

Solution One: Institutionalization and Ministry

The Church as Institution

The first major response of the author to the situation of his church(es) is institutionalization. Margaret MacDonald has shown that institutionalization is present from the very beginning of the church's life. She styles the work of the historical Paul as that of community-building institutionalization, the task of Colossians and Ephesians as community-stabilizing institutionalization, and the goal of the Pastoral Epistles as community-protecting institutionalization. She identifies a cumulative process of institutionalization in the life cycle of the Pauline churches.[32]

MacDonald concludes that the circumstances faced by many of the churches toward the end of the first and the beginning of the second centuries forced them to tighten leadership structures. "The legitimation of the authority of officials became the primary means of ensuring the continued existence of communities."[33] One can observe that process in the household codes of Colossians and Ephesians, where power is put more firmly into the hands of those in leadership, a tendency that is that much more pronounced in the later "Pastoral Epistles, where household ethics and the delineation of criteria for determining who is eligible for leadership positions go hand in hand."[34] Indeed, household codes are found in Titus 2:1-10 and mixed with codes on church order in 1 Tim. 2:1—6:2.

Ministry

Ministry of the Word.   The author sought to meet the needs of his congregations by giving attention to three aspects of congregational life: ministry, the place of women, and the relationship of the church to society.

One of the most distinctive ways the author responded is through his understanding of ministry. As opposed to the undisputed letters, in which every Christian has a *charisma* or gift of the Spirit (Rom. 1:11; 12:6; 1 Cor. 7:7; 12:4), in the Pastorals the word *charisma* is linked with holding office and the laying on of hands (1 Tim. 4:14; 2 Tim. 1:6). Hanson suggests that comparing 2 Tim. 1:6-9 with Rom. 8:12-17 is especially instructive: what in Romans refers to all Christians is in 2 Timothy applied to the church leader only.

The officeholders are intimately connected with the Word of God, as is seen in 2 Tim. 2:8-9. Paul goes on to direct Timothy, "Do your best to present yourself to God as one approved by him, a worker who has no need to be ashamed, rightly explaining the word of truth" (2:15). A better translation of the last phrase is "cutting straight the word of truth" (*orthotomeō*). The term referred originally to cutting a path or road in a straight direction. It also means to cut correctly (*orthōs*). Timothy is also directed to "preach the word" (4:2, RSV; NRSV "proclaim the message"), having been encouraged by the example of Paul, who was able even during imprisonment to proclaim the message (4:17). The ability to carry out similar proclamation depends on God's initiating word and the giving of that word to an authorized representative (Titus 1:3). The bishop, therefore, "must have a firm grasp of the word that is trustworthy in accordance with the teaching" (1:9). "Nourished on the words of the faith" (1 Tim. 4:6), the church leader is able to oppose those whose word (NRSV "talk") eats like gangrene (2 Tim. 2:17) and is able to instruct other believers "so that the word of God may not be discredited" (Titus 2:5).

The designated leaders are also directed to use Scripture, which "is inspired by God and is useful for teaching, for reproof, for correction, and for training in righteousness" (2 Tim. 3:16). The function of Scripture is related directly to its use by the officeholders: "so that the man of God [NRSV incorrectly translates the Greek as 'everyone who belongs to God'] may be proficient, equipped for every good work" (2 Tim. 3:17). The emphasis is on the usefulness of the God-inspired Scriptures for ministry.

Ministry in the Pastorals is thus closely tied to the Word of God. The exact organization of that ministry is, however, unclear.

Bishop. The relationship between the bishop and the elder (presbyter) is hard to delineate. A key datum is that the term "bishop" occurs only in the singular (1 Tim. 3:2; Titus 1:7), whereas the term "elder" occurs in the plural. A second datum is that the qualifications for the two offices are quite similar, as are many of the duties (note the ease with which the author passes from elder to bishop, Titus 1:5-9). The two terms most likely represent the fusion of two church orders. The churches of Paul did not have elders, but at least in Philippi they had bishops (Phil. 1:1). In contrast, Palestinian Christianity had adopted leadership patterns from the synagogue, which was governed by elders. In the Pastorals the two systems are fused. The churches of the Pastorals may also have looked to the diaspora synagogues, which were governed by a leader (*archisynagōgos*) and a board of elders (*gerousia*). They, in turn, were helped by the assistants (*diakonoi*).

First Timothy 4:14 also mentions a "council of elders" or "presbytery." The most probable explanation is that the one bishop was chosen from the council of elders. For that reason the qualifications for both offices are the same, and for that reason "bishop" is in the singular. At the same time, it is improbable that the Pastorals refer to a monarchical bishop. The first clear evidence for that office is Ignatius of Antioch.

The term "bishop" or "overseer" had currency both inside and outside Judaism. The term is often studied in relationship to the Hebrew word *mebaqqer* ("overseer"), which was used at Qumran for the persons who presided over the community. They supervised care of the poor as well as admission of persons into the community. They also preached and taught.[35] Outside Judaism, the Greek term *episkopos* referred to a person who had supervisory authority. In the Pastorals the bishop is to manage the household congregation in a way analogous to the management of his own personal household (1 Tim. 3:1-7). Designation of the bishop as "God's steward" (or "household manager," *oikonomos*, Titus 1:7) indicates his financial responsibilities (cf. 1 Tim. 3:3). He is to be a bastion of truth over against the falsehood of the opponents (Titus 1:9; 1 Tim. 3:6). He is also to be skilled in teaching (1 Tim. 3:2; Titus 1:9), an important function especially when false teachings abound.

Elder. For the elder we have more data. "Let the elders who rule well be considered worthy of double honor, especially those who labor in preaching and teaching" (1 Tim. 5:17). To "rule well" means to exercise good leadership. "Double honor" most likely refers to double payment (the word for "honor," *timē*, is often used for financial payment). We once more encounter preaching and teaching as functions of office, but only for some elders. The others engage in administrative activities only. Verse 18 provides scriptural support for the payment of religious leaders. Verses 19-21 lay out procedures regarding discipline. Verse 22 reminds Timothy not to ordain hastily. Verses 24-25 remind Timothy that in this world one cannot be sure whether disciplinary or ordination decisions are right: some misdeeds are obvious, others are not. The hope is that good deeds cannot, ultimately, remain hidden.[36] In Titus 1:5, Titus is to appoint elders in every town where a congregation is established, and in 1 Tim. 4:14 the elders form a council that is involved in ordaining others such as Timothy (whose specific title is not mentioned).

The term "elder" has its home in the OT and Judaism, where it designated those of great age. The title was extended to those who held office, who were often older (e.g., Num. 11:16-25). In the NT the Sanhedrin and the councils of local synagogues included elders, and that pattern was carried over into parts of the early church (Acts 15:2, 4, 6, 22-23; 16:4; 21:18; James 5:14; 1 Pet. 5:1-4). Advanced age is not a criterion in the Pastorals for being an "elder," since an elder can still have children young enough to be under his authority (Titus 1:6). In addition, the counsel to Timothy to "let no one despise your youth" (1 Tim. 4:12) may be directed against age requirements, although admittedly Timothy is never called an elder (perhaps because he was itinerant).

The congregations of the Pastorals practiced the laying on of hands as the method of ordination (1 Tim. 5:22; 4:14). Ordination was preceded by a charismatic selection process (1 Tim. 1:18; 4:14). The ordinands were instructed (2 Tim. 3:14-17) and in some way tested or evaluated (1 Tim. 5:22; 2 Tim. 2:2). The ceremony itself included prayer and the laying on of hands (1 Tim. 4:14). The *charisma* given in ordination was not magic: it could be neglected (1 Tim. 4:14) and therefore needed to be rekindled (2 Tim. 1:6). At the heart of ordination in the Pastorals is the public recognition and authorization of the ordinand to guard and pass on the deposit of faith.[37]

Deacon.   The third office is the deacon. The term itself means "servant" (*diakonos*) and is closely associated with the bishop both in 1 Tim. 3:1-13 and in Phil. 1:1. The exact duties of the deacons are not detailed. The term was used outside the church for a person with a subordinate function. The deacons are to be tested before assuming their office (1 Tim. 3:10), and "they must hold fast to the mystery of the faith with a clear conscience" (3:9).

Were there female as well as male deacons? The section on deacons (1 Tim. 3:8-13) has this sentence: "Women [or 'wives'; the Greek word can be translated either way] likewise must be serious, not slanderers, but temperate, faithful in all things" (v. 11). In antiquity Ambrosiaster and in modern times Easton, Jeremias, Hanson, and Verner have understood the passage to mean "their wives," that is, the wives of the deacons. But also in antiquity Theodoret and Theodore of Mopsuestia took another position, followed by the modern commentators Spicq, Hultgren (with some hesitation), Kelly, Karris, and Roloff: the verse refers to female deacons. Verses 8-10 are on deacons in general, verse 11 is on female deacons, and verses 12-13 are on male deacons. Although that outline is a bit awkward, the use of "likewise" in verses 8 and 11 seems to be the author's way of introducing new categories. In addition, there was no special word in the late first century for "deaconess"; the one word covered both males and females. One can conclude, tentatively, that the churches of the Pastorals had female deacons.

Widow.   Women's ministry is clearly the topic in 1 Tim. 5:3-16. Verses 4 and 8 remind families to care for their own widows. Those who had families needed to be supported by them so that the congregation would be able to help widows who had no such hope of support (v. 16). The widows are also to be "above reproach," verse 7, the same word applied to bishops (3:2).

While verses 3-8 may deal with an order of widows, verses 9-15 definitely discuss a formally constituted office of widows. Verse 9a details the official enrollment of widows who meet certain qualifications (vv. 9b-10), while verse 11 calls for the rejection of younger widows. The language in verses 9 and 11 likely refers to "voting in" and "voting down."[38] Another indication of the existence of an office of widows is the list of requirements, which resembles the comparable lists for other offices in the Pastorals.

1. A male officeholder is to be the husband of one wife (1 Tim. 3:2, 12; Titus 1:6); an enrolled widow is to be the wife of one husband (1 Tim. 5:9).

2. A male officeholder is to be hospitable (1 Tim. 3:2; Titus 1:8); the widow, too, is to be well attested in showing hospitality (1 Tim. 5:10).

3. The man is to take proper care of his children (1 Tim. 3:4, 12; Titus 1:6); so is the widow (1 Tim. 5:10).

Supporting evidence comes from documents written in the same geographical area within a relatively short time of the writing of the Pastorals (Ign. *Smyrn.* 13.1; Ign. *Pol.* 4.1; Pol. *Phil.* 4.5; 5.3).

What did the widows do? In verse 5, the "real widow" prays night and day. Verse 10 mentions activities such as rearing children, washing the feet of the saints, and supporting the afflicted; those activities, however, are listed as *prior* qualifications, not necessarily duties of the enrolled widow. Kelly sees them as the sort of duties expected of the enrolled widows, but Thurston denies that these "activities" are activities at all. She argues that each of them represents a spiritual quality.

Only older women are to hold the office, although verses 11-12 show that a different approach had been taken at one time. The presence of younger women among the widows troubles the author so much that he counsels remarriage, which would eliminate them from ever becoming part of the office of widow (vv. 11 and 14). The way to control the younger widows is to have them married rather than giving them official status as widows.[39] In structuring an order of widows, the author has sought to bring under control (from his perspective) a troublesome group.

Titus 2:3-5 outlines qualities and duties for a group called "the older women." They are to be reverent, not slanderers, nor enslaved to drink. They are to be teachers of what is good, with the goal of training the young women to love their husbands and children, be self-controlled, chaste, domestic, kind, and submissive to their husbands (v. 4). Whether one should equate the "older women" of Titus 2 with the widows of 1 Timothy 5 is unclear.

Qualifications of Officeholders.   The Pastoral Epistles devote much space to the personal qualifications of officeholders. 1 Tim. 3:1-7 is a good example. From it we learn four things about qualifications for office.

1. The qualifications are not specifically Christian. Almost every term can be paralleled elsewhere in Hellenistic literature, particularly in lists of duties for various occupations. The personal qualifications are not created in a vacuum but are essentially adopted from society.[40]

2. The key qualification is that the officeholder be "above reproach" (*anepilēmpton*). The term stands at the head of the list of qualifications and is the guiding principle (see also 1 Tim. 5:7; 6:14). It is resumed in verse 7 with the reference to a good witness or reputation (*martyria*; NRSV "be well thought of") with outsiders. The word occurs regularly in Hellenistic duty lists. Related is the term "blameless" (Titus 1:6-7; 1 Tim. 3:10).

3. The first example of living "above reproach" is the bishop's marital life. The Greek reads "the husband of one wife" (so RSV), the exact meaning of which is unclear. The options are: not a polygamist; never divorced; has not remarried, whether widowed or divorced. What is indisputable is the significance of marriage in the church orders of the Pastorals (see also 1 Tim. 3:12; 5:9; Titus 1:6). Such a requirement finds no parallel in other Hellenistic lists of duties.

4. Another unique qualification and one that is skill related is that the bishop is to be "an apt teacher" (in Greek, "skillful in teaching"). This qualification also does not occur widely in Hellenistic literature.[41]

Besides the qualifications listed for specific offices, numerous qualifications are detailed for the paradigmatic figures Timothy and Titus. Timothy is to be "nourished on the words of the faith and of the sound teaching" that he has followed (1 Tim. 4:6). He is reminded not to neglect the gift given to him through prophecy and the laying on of hands (4:14; 2 Tim. 1:6). He is also advised to "pay close attention to yourself and to your teaching" (1 Tim. 4:16). The need for self-care of the minister is not a recent discovery.

Tasks of the Officeholders. Possible duties of the widows have already been discussed. When directions to Timothy and Titus as well as the picture of Paul are included, a partial picture emerges for the other officeholders, too.

Paul has been entrusted with the gospel (1 Tim. 1:11). Timothy, in turn, is to have faith (1:19) and "keep the commandment without spot or blame" (6:14). Even more, Timothy is to "guard what has been entrusted" to him (6:20; 2 Tim. 1:13-14; 2:14-15; 3:14; 4:1-5; Titus 1:9). Even though ultimately God does the guarding (2 Tim. 1:12), Timothy also must "guard the good treasure [or 'deposit'] entrusted" to him, being strengthened by the Holy Spirit (1:14). Timothy is also to entrust the tradition to others who themselves will be able to teach those who follow them (2:2; cf. Titus 1:5). The chain of succession is not one of office but of tradition (as contrasted with *1 Clement* 42 and 44). Timothy and his successors are to preserve the sound teaching (1 Tim. 1:10; 2 Tim. 4:3; Titus 1:9, 2:1) and pass it on. The deposit is not a lifeless body of dogma but a living body of teaching that is to be proclaimed and that includes inspired interpretation of the Scriptures (2 Tim. 3:14-17; 4:1-5; see comments above on ministry of the Word).

Implicit in the need to guard the deposit is the battle to which the officeholder is called. Timothy is to fight the good fight of the faith (1 Tim. 1:18; 6:12 [vv. 11-16 are probably a charge to the newly ordained]; 2 Tim. 2:3-4). The image of the soldier or athlete (1 Tim. 4:7b; 2 Tim.

2:5; cf. Phil. 2:25; 3:12-14; Philem. 2) is common in philosophical diatribes and highlights the dedication needed.[42] The officeholder and other Christians can anticipate suffering (2 Tim. 1:8; 2:3, 11-13; 3:10-12; 4:5), which is based on the model of Paul (1:8-12; 2:9-10), whose struggle is almost over (4:6-8).

In addition to the judicial and administrative responsibilities outlined for church leaders (1 Tim. 3:4-5; 5:19-22), Timothy is to be an example to other believers, regardless of his youth (4:12; cf. 1 Cor. 16:11). So is Titus (Titus 2:7-8; cf. Paul in 1 Cor. 11:1; Phil. 3:17; 1 Thess. 1:6-7).

The variety and breadth of the ministerial tasks are illustrated by the outlines for ministry contained in 1 Tim. 4:11-16 and 2 Tim. 4:2-5. What is absent from such lists, as from the Pastorals in general, is any priestly function for the officeholders, including presiding at Eucharist (despite Hanson's creative comments on 1 Tim. 2:1, 8 [the one real possibility]; 4:5; 2 Tim. 1:10). That the author has used liturgical materials[43] makes the omission of eucharistic references even more striking.

In these letters we see the beginnings of standards of conduct for holding office, as well as the beginning of a break with the earlier Christian pattern of authority resident in the head of the household because the person was the head of the household. Some of that approach still remains, but with the figure of Timothy we have also seen that expertise, training, and conduct are becoming criteria independent of one's age or traditional position within the community. The transitional point evident in the Pastorals is illustrated by the charismatic Christian prophets (1 Tim. 4:14; see also 1:18), who still have a say in choosing ordinands but who do not themselves constitute an office. Original charismatic authority (prophecy) and organizational structure (bishop and presbytery) coexist at the time of the writing of these documents.[44]

Early Catholicism?   The Pastoral Epistles have often been viewed as representing a steep decline from the theological heights of Paul. Their emphasis on institution and office signal for some the beginning of "early catholicism." Perhaps the most strident figure is Käsemann.[45] In his model, all Christians in Paul's communities were charismatic ministers. When those communities (especially in Asia Minor) were threatened by Gnosticism following Paul's death, however, they forfeited their nature as Pauline communities for legally defined structure. The offices evident in the Pastoral Epistles led directly to the monarchical bishop who, for Käsemann, is the opposite of Paul's intention.[46]

But sheer establishment of offices does not constitute early catholicism. The development of more formalized offices is, from a sociological perspective, a natural growth in the development of a religious organization.

That tendency was furthered by the threat of heresy, as the church found it necessary to establish offices that were able to take responsibility for the right proclamation of the gospel. As we have seen, the chief leadership offices are dedicated to the preservation of the Word. That is, we have in the Pastorals the priority of the Word vis-à-vis the office, a relationship opposite that of early catholicism, as usually defined, in which the office is dominant. Nor, as we have discovered, are the offices defined in cultic terms. The letters may well be on a trajectory that is taken by others in the direction of early catholicism, but early catholicism is not a necessary conclusion to be drawn from the theology of the Pastorals.

Solution Two: Accommodation

Women

The second major response by the author to the situation of his churches is accommodation with society. One form of accommodation is his perspective on women, as illustrated by 1 Tim. 2:8-15.

The overriding concern in 1 Timothy 2 is order within the community. For that reason, only men are to pray (v. 8). In verses 11-12 the author turns to women's roles. Women are, first, to learn "in silence with full submission." The women here *are* to learn, but they are to be submissive to the male teachers. Moreover, they are not to dominate the men ("have authority over a man") nor to teach them. Rather, the women are to be silent. The reasons given in support are twofold. First, Adam was created before Eve and thus has priority. Second, and more significant in the author's argument, is that sin is traced to "the woman." The author adopts here not the tradition used by Paul in Romans 5—sin goes back to Adam—but that used in Sir. 25:24—sin begins with Eve. Eve was deceived; Adam was not. In verse 15, how is a Christian woman saved by bearing children? She is saved not by the sheer procreative act but by fulfilling the societal role assigned to her, that of wife and mother. A similar position is taken in Titus 2:3-5.

The kind of thinking that these letters oppose may account in part for the author's attitude toward women. In Gnosticism, procreation was considered evil, with the result that marriage and family life were denigrated (1 Tim. 4:3). D. MacDonald's thesis of the *Acts of Paul and Thecla* may also figure in here. Finally, the need for the author to carve out a positive societal niche for Christianity may have led to his perspective on women. The text shows that Christian women fulfill traditional roles that support society.

Accommodation with Society

The emphasis on piety or godliness, prayer for rulers, acceptance of wealth, and adoption of societal standards for leadership and for the place of women have been understood as indications of accommodation by the author to his society. Christianity is thereby presented to the surrounding society as supportive of society and therefore "safe." Thus directions are given only to slaves in 1 Tim. 6:1-2, with nothing being said to the masters (contrast Philemon and Eph. 6:9). In general, the use of household station codes adopted from the society indicates increased conformity with Greco-Roman values.

Sociologists often classify early Christianity as a conversionist sect. Such a sect has a dialectical relationship with the outside world: it wants to convert people from the broader society and so must not appear too strange, but it also needs to maintain its distinctiveness if it is to have a unique message to proclaim.[47] Building on such insights, Wallis places religious groups along a continuum of world-affirming, world-accommodating, and world-rejecting positions.[48] Dealing with societal factors forces the group to clarify its world perspective and thus to solidify its position on the continuum or move it in one direction or the other.

Most sects begin at a world-rejecting position. From a sociological perspective, the movement away from that position is accommodation and is caused by several factors, the key one being response to social disapproval. "New sects which experience opposition . . . do so largely because their practices seem to threaten established and respected social norms or institutions such as the family."[49] For some groups disapproval by the society reaffirms the group's self-identity as a minority; for other groups disapproval by the broader society may be experienced as more threatening. In its reaction to groups perceived as deviant, the society seeks to control them by encouraging them to adopt attitudes and behavior more consistent with the dominant society.

The author of the Pastorals represents in many ways a world-accommodating religion: he has accommodated many of his views to the surrounding culture in order to make communication and evangelism possible. He has also moved in that direction because of perceived threats from the society. Sociologists teach that such movement is not necessarily bad. The question to be asked of the Pastorals is at what cost the accommodation was made. One cost was certainly the leadership role of women.

The Witness of the Pastoral Epistles

As I noted at the beginning, the Pastoral Epistles at times have been evaluated negatively. Yet they are of great importance for understanding the growing institutionalization of the church toward the end of the first century. In many ways they charted the trajectory that the church took in succeeding centuries, and they are at the center of contemporary discussions of ministry and the place of women within the church.

The Pastorals also present their own peculiar witness, within the Pauline tradition, to the good news of Jesus Christ. We have seen that Titus 2:11-14 is the proposition, or theme, of the three letters. With that passage as a guide, I summarize the witness of the Pastorals as follows.

1. "The grace of God has *appeared* [*epephanē*] . . . ; we wait for . . . the *manifestation* [*epiphaneian*] of the glory of . . . Jesus Christ." Christian life is lived in between: in between the first epiphany of Jesus and his second epiphany.

2. That grace of God has appeared, "bringing *salvation* to all," because Jesus is "our great God and *Savior*, . . . who gave himself for us." God's desire is that everyone will be saved and come to the knowledge of the truth (1 Tim. 2:4), and so Jesus came to save (1 Tim. 1:15).

3. The grace of God *trains* (*paideuousa*) or educates us "in the present age to live lives" within a tension that calls us "to renounce impiety and worldly passions," on the one hand, and to live "self-controlled, upright, and godly" lives, on the other, as "a people of his own," whom he has redeemed and purified for himself. For the author of the Pastorals, living "in the present age" presumes the basic goodness of creation, including married life, family life, and societal life.

4. In the grace of God, we as Christ's people are also to be "zealous for *good deeds*." Thus life in the present age is structured to reflect God's call, whether that life be the life of the Christian within society as she or he seeks to witness to the saving activity of God; whether that life be in the family, as family members witness to God's grace; or whether that life be in the official ministries of the church, as the leaders embody the ideals of the church, encourage them in others, and represent the church to the surrounding society and to intrachurch opponents.

5. All of the above can happen because of "the *grace* of God," "who saved us and called us with a holy calling, not according to our works but according to his own purpose and grace" (2 Tim. 1:9).

Notes

1. Since all theories of authorship posit a male author, the author is identified generically as "he."

2. The position has been worked out most carefully by Jerome D. Quinn, "P⁴⁶— the Pauline Canon?" *CBQ* 36 (1974): 379–85.

3. "Undisputed letters" is a term that designates Romans, 1 and 2 Corinthians, Galatians, Philippians, 1 Thessalonians, and Philemon, letters about which there is no question regarding authorship by the historical Paul.

4. Robert Morgenthaler, *Statistik des neutestamentlichen Wortschatzes* (Zurich: Gotthelf, 1958), 28, 38.

5. All of this is evidence for Beker of the author's "bifurcation of coherence and contingency," which "produces a linguistic structure that petrifies Paul's dynamic coherent language and thus relates itself only artificially to its contingent situation. In fact Paul's concepts have now become sacrosanct and 'holy' words to which the tradition has given a fixed and frozen meaning. And so they have lost their dynamic interrelation with the particular contingent situation in and for which they originally functioned" (J. Christiaan Beker, *Heirs of Paul: Paul's Legacy in the New Testament and in the Church Today* [Minneapolis: Fortress, 1991], 41).

6. Klaus Beyer, *Semitische Syntax im Neuen Testament* I. 1, SUNT 1 (Göttingen: Vandenhoeck & Ruprecht, 1962), 232, 295, 298.

7. Bruce M. Metzger, "A Reconsideration of Certain Arguments Against the Pauline Authorship of the Pastoral Epistles," *Exp Tim* 70 (1958/59): 91–94; Donald Guthrie, *The Pastoral Epistles*, Tyndale New Testament Commentaries, rev. ed. (Grand Rapids: Eerdmans, 1990), 224–40.

8. A. T. Hanson, *The Pastoral Epistles*, NCBC (Grand Rapids: Eerdmans, 1982), 28; see his chart on p. 199.

9. For an opposing opinion, see Luke T. Johnson, *The Writings of the New Testament: An Interpretation* (Philadelphia: Fortress, 1986), 384–85.

10. The NRSV's "instruct" is too weak. The word is a military term for giving orders.

11. For extensive discussions of "save" and "savior" in the Pastorals, see Jerome D. Quinn, *The Letter to Titus* AB 35 (New York: Doubleday, 1990), 304–15; and Martin Dibelius and Hans Conzelmann, *The Pastoral Epistles*, trans. Philip Buttolph and Adela Yarbro, Hermeneia (Philadelphia: Fortress, 1972), 100–103.

12. Quinn (*Titus*, 282–90) contains a helpful excursus on the term and its cognates.

13. It is of some note that the major passages, 1 Tim. 4:1 and 2 Tim. 3:1, occur at a comparable place in their respective books, i.e., starting the second half.

14. Johnson, 391.

15. E. Randolph Richards (*The Secretary in the Letters of Paul*, WUNT 2.42 [Tübingen: Mohr-Siebeck 1991], 1, 11) suggests that the heretofore common designation of a document's secretary as the "amanuensis" be dropped. Amaneunsis, his research shows, is too rare and too narrow a term to bear the weight often assigned it. He recommends "secretary" as the designation.

16. C. F. D. Moule ("The Problem of the Pastoral Epistles: A Reappraisal," *BJRL* 47 [1965]: 442–46) provides a detailed listing of similarities in vocabulary.

17. Ibid., 440.

18. Jürgen Roloff, *Der Erste Brief an Timotheus*, EKKNT 15 (Zurich: Benziger; Neukirchen-Vluyn: Neukirchener, 1988), 32; Robert J. Karris, *The Pastoral Epistles*, New Testament Message 17 (Wilmington, Del.: Glazier, 1979), 41–42; Lewis R. Donelson, *Pseudepigraphy and Ethical Argument in the Pastoral Epistles* HUT 22 (Tübingen: Mohr-Siebeck, 1986), 56–57.

19. John L. White, *Light from Ancient Letters*, Foundations and Facets (Philadelphia: Fortress, 1986), 189–90. Donelson develops in detail the characteristic features of Greco-Roman pseudepigraphic letters (23–54), and Benjamin Fiore (*The Function of Personal Example in the Socratic and Pastoral Epistles*, AnBib 105 [Rome: Biblical Institute Press, 1986] has demonstrated the many parallels in genre and method between the Socratic Epistles and the Pastoral Epistles.

20. Donelson, 54; see the entire section, pp. 54–66, and Fiore, 233–34.

21. C. K. Barrett, *The Pastoral Epistles in the New English Bible with Introduction and Commentary* (Oxford: Clarendon, 1963), 57; David C. Verner, *The Household of God: The Social World of the Pastoral Epistles*, SBLDS 71 (Chico, Calif.: Scholars Press, 1983), 151; Joachim Jeremias, *Die Briefe an Timotheus und Titus*, NTD 9, 4th ed. (Göttingen: Vandenhoeck & Ruprecht, 1975), 33–34.

22. See, e.g., Floyd Filson, "The Significance of the Early House Churches," *JBL* 58 (1939): 111–12; Bengt Holmberg, *Paul and Power: The Structure of Authority in the Primitive Church as Reflected in the Pauline Epistles* (Philadelphia: Fortress, 1978) 105. Abraham J. Malherbe argues against such a conclusion (*Social Aspects of Early Christianity*, 2d ed., enlarged [Philadelphia: Fortress, 1983], 99).

23. See Gerd Theissen, *The Social Setting of Pauline Christianity: Essays on Corinth*, ed. and trans. John H. Schütz (Philadelphia: Fortress, 1982); Walter F. Taylor, Jr., "Sociological Exegesis: Introduction to a New Way to Study the Bible. Part II: Results," *Trinity Seminary Review* 12 (1990): 29–34. On the benefactor-client system in the Pastorals see Reggie M. Kidd, *Wealth and Beneficence in the Pastoral Epistles*, SBLDS 122 (Atlanta: Scholars Press, 1990), 39, 53–55, 60.

24. See also the *Treatise on the Resurrection* I. 4, 48–49, from Nag Hammadi; contrast 2 Tim. 2:11, where the reference is to a future living with Jesus.

25. On the Gnostic phrase "knowledge of the truth," see Quinn, *Titus*, 282; and Jesse Sell, *The Knowledge of the Truth—Two Doctrines*, European University Studies Series 23, vol. 194 (Frankfurt am Main: Peter Lang, 1982). On the Gnostic concern with genealogies see, e.g., *On the Origin of the World*, II.5, 98–102; Irenaeus *Against Heresies* 1.30.9.

26. Another possibility is that there are several distinct groups of opponents. See John Reumann, *Variety and Unity in New Testament Thought*, (Oxford Bible Study Series (Oxford: Oxford Univ. Press, 1991) 135.

27. Robert L. Wilken, "The Christians as the Romans (and Greeks) Saw Them," in *Jewish and Christian Self-Understanding*, ed. E. P. Sanders, vol. 1: *The Shaping of Christianity in the Second and Third Centuries* (Philadelphia: Fortress, 1980), 100–25; idem, *The Christians as the Romans Saw Them* (New Haven and London: Yale Univ. Press, 1984), 15–28, 48–67, 117–25. See also Wayne A. Meeks, *The First Urban Christians: The Social World of the Apostle Paul* (New Haven and London: Yale Univ. Press, 1983), 106.

28. David L. Balch, *Let Wives Be Submissive: The Domestic Code in I Peter*, SBLMS 26 (Chico, Calif.: Scholars Press, 1981), 14–15, 24, 29, 40–43, 51–52, 46, 61–62; John H. Elliott, *A Home for the Homeless: A Sociological Exegesis of 1 Peter, Its Situation and Strategy* (Philadelphia: Fortress, 1981) 167–87, 213–19; E. A. Judge, *The Social Pattern of the Christian Groups in the First Century* (London: Tyndale, 1960), 30–38; Dieter Lührmann, "Neutestamentliche Haustafeln und antike Ökonomie," *NTS* 27 (1980/81) 85–90.

29. Walter Bauer, *Orthodoxy and Heresy in Earliest Christianity* (Philadelphia: Fortress, 1971), 222-28; Hans von Campenhausen, "Polykarp von Smyrna und die Pastoralbriefe," in *Aus der Frühzeit des Christentums* (Tübingen: Mohr-Siebeck, 1963), 197–252.

30. Selected scholars and their suggested writing dates: Fuller, 65–90; Hanson, 90–110; Quinn, 80–85; Roloff, 80–100.

31. William J. Beckwith, "Faithful Is the Word: The Cynic Epistolary Corpus and the Purpose of the Pastorals" and "Behavior in the Household of God: Rhetorical

Structure and the Social World of the Pastoral Epistles" (Unpublished manuscripts; Trinity Lutheran Seminary, 1987).

32. Margaret Y. MacDonald, *The Pauline Churches: A Socio-historical Study of Institutionalization in the Pauline and Deutero-Pauline Writings* (SNTSMS 60 (Cambridge: Cambridge Univ. Press, 1988), 31–234.

33. Ibid., 136.

34. Ibid., 137.

35. B. E. Thiering, "*Mebaqqer* and *Episkopos* in the Light of the Temple Scroll," *JBL* 100 (1981): 59–74.

36. J. P. Meier, "*Presbyteros* in the Pastoral Epistles," *CBQ* 35 (1973): 323–45.

37. See Eduard Lohse, *Die Ordination im Spätjudentum und im Neuen Testament* (Göttingen: Vandenhoeck & Ruprecht, 1951); G. Lohfink, "Die Normativität der Amtsvorstellungen in den Pastoralbriefen," *TQ* 157 (1977): 93–106; Heinrich Schlier, "Die Ordnung der Kirche nach den Pastoralbriefen," in *Das kirchliche Amt im Neuen Testament*, ed. Karl Kertelge (Darmstadt: Wissenschaftliche Buchgesellschaft, 1977), 475–500.

38. Gustav Stählin, "*chēra*," *TDNT* 9:456–57.

39. The qualities required in 1 Timothy 5 of the older woman are quite similar to those in 1 Tim. 3:11 for the female deacon. Not much later the offices of female deacon and widow were equated. Thurston points out that it is difficult to trace the history of either concept, because the terms so early became confused with each other (Bonnie Bowman Thurston, *The Widows: A Women's Ministry in the Early Church* [Minneapolis: Fortress, 1989], 52).

40. Dibelius-Conzelmann, 50–51. See, e.g., Onosander's list of qualities needed by the general (ca. A.D. 50), in ibid., 158–60; and Roland Schwarz, *Bürgerliches Christentum im Neuen Testament? Eine Studie zu Ethik, Amt und Recht in den Pastoralbriefen* (Klosterneuburg: Österreichische Katholisches Bibelwerk, 1983), 34–61.

41. For more on 1 Tim. 3:1-7 see Walter F. Taylor, Jr., "1 Timothy 3:1-7: The Public Side of Ministry," *Trinity Seminary Review* 14 (1992): 5–17.

42. See Victor C. Pfitzner, *Paul and the Agon Motif: Traditional Athletic Imagery in the Pauline Literature*, TSup 16 (Leiden: Brill, 1967), 165–85.

43. Quinn, *Titus*, 10.

44. For more on sociological theories of office, see Max Weber, *The Theory of Social and Economic Organization*, trans. A. M. Henderson and Talcott Parsons; ed. with an Introduction by Talcott Parsons (Glencoe, Ill.: Free Press, 1947); idem, *The Sociology of Religion*, ed. Ephraim Fischoff, with an Introduction by Talcott Parsons (London: Methuen, 1966); Wolfgang Schluchter, "Einleitung: Max Webers Analyse des antiken Christentums. Grundzüge eines unvollendeten Projekts," in *Max Webers Sicht des antiken Christentums: Interpretation und Kritik*, ed. Wolfgang Schluchter, Suhrkamp-Taschenbuch Wissenschaft 548 (Frankfurt: Suhrkamp, 1985), 11–72; Walter F. Taylor, Jr., "Sociological Exegesis: Introduction to a New Way to Study the Bible. Part I," *Trinity Seminary Review* 11 (1989): 102–4; idem, "1 Tim. 3:1-7."

45. Ernst Käsemann, "Ministry and Community in the New Testament," in *Essays on New Testament Themes*, trans. W. J. Montague, SBT 1/41 (London: SCM, 1964), 63–94; idem, "Paul and Early Catholicism," in *New Testament Questions of Today*, trans. W. J. Montague (London: SCM, 1969), 236–51.

46. A similar position is taken by Eduard Schweizer, *Church Order in the New Testament*, trans. Frank Clarke, (SBT 1/32 (London: SCM, 1961): 85–86.

47. Bryan Wilson, "An Analysis of Sect Development," *American Sociological Review* 24 (1959): 9–10, 12; reprinted in *Patterns of Sectarianism: Organisation and Ideology in Social and Religious Movements*, ed. Bryan R. Wilson (London: Heinemann, 1967), 34–35, 39–40. For reservations about the sect model, see Bengt Holmberg, *Sociology and the New Testament: An Appraisal* (Minneapolis: Fortress, 1990), 90–91, 108–14, who nevertheless makes positive comments about the application of the conversionist sect label, 93–96 (but see also 113).

48. Roy Wallis, *The Elementary Forms of the New Religious Life*, International Library of Sociology (London: Routledge & Kegan Paul, 1984), 9–39, 73–85, 119–31.

49. Annette P. Hampshire and James A. Beckford, "Religious Sects and the Concept of Deviance: The Moonies and the Mormons," *British Journal of Sociology* 34 (1983): 225; Thomas Robbins, "Cults, Converts and Charisma: The Sociology of New Religious Movements," *Current Sociology* 36 (1988): 115.

SELECTED BIBLIOGRAPHIES

Ephesians

Abbott, T. K. *Epistles to the Ephesians and to the Colossians.* ICC Edinburgh: T. & T. Clark, 1897.

Arnold, Clinton E. *Ephesians: Power & Magic: The Concept of Power in Ephesians in the Light of Its Historical Setting.* SNTSMS 63. Cambridge: Cambridge Univ. Press, 1989.

Barth, Markus. *Ephesians: Introduction, Translation and Commentary.* AB 34, 34A. 2 vols. Garden City, N.Y.: Doubleday, 1974.

Bruce, F. F. *The Epistles to the Colossians, to Philemon, and to the Ephesians.* NICNT. Rev. ed. Grand Rapids: Eerdmans, 1984.

Caird, G. B. *Paul's Letters from Prison.* London: Oxford Univ. Press, 1976.

Collins, R. F. *Letters That Paul Did Not Write: The Epistle to the Hebrews and the Pauline Pseudepigrapha.* Wilmington, Del.: Michael Glazier; Collegeville, Minn.: Liturgical Press, 1988.

Culpepper, A. "Ethical Dualism and Church Discipline, Eph. 4:25—5:20." *RevExp* 76 (1978): 529–39.

Goodspeed, E. J. *The Meaning of Ephesians.* Chicago: University of Chicago Press, 1933.

Lincoln, Andrew T. *Ephesians.* WBC 42. Dallas: Word, 1990.

———. "The Use of the Old Testament in Ephesians." *JSNT* 14 (1982): 16–57.

MacDonald, M. Y. *The Pauline Churches: A Socio-historical Study of Institutionalization in the Pauline and Deutro-Pauline Writings.* SNTSMS 60. Cambridge: Cambridge Univ. Press, 1983.

Mitton, C. Leslie. *Ephesians.* NCBC. Grand Rapids: Eerdmans, 1981.

Patzia, Arthur G. *Ephesians, Colossians, Philemon.* New International Biblical Commentary. Peabody, Mass.: Hendrickson, 1991.

Sampley, J. Paul. *"And the Two Shall Become One Flesh": A Study of Traditions in Ephesians 5:21-33.* Cambridge: Cambridge Univ. Press, 1971.

Scott, E. F. *The Epistles of Paul to the Colossians, to Philemon and to the Ephesians.* MNTC. New York: Harper, 1930.

Wild, R. A. "The Warrior and the Prisoner: Some Reflections on Ephesians 6:10-20." *CBQ* 46 (1984): 284–98.

Colossians

Bruce, F. F. *The Epistles to the Colossians, to Philemon, and to the Ephesians.* NICNT. Rev. ed. Grand Rapids: Eerdmans, 1984.

Bujard, Walter. *Stilanalytische Untersuchungen zum Kolosserbrief als Beitrag zur Methodik von Sprachvergleichen.* SUNT 11. Göttingen: Vandenhoeck & Ruprecht, 1973.

Crouch, James E. *The Origin and Intention of the Colossian Haustafel.* FRLANT 109. Göttingen: Vandenhoeck & Ruprecht, 1972.

Francis, Fred O., and Wayne A. Mecks, eds. *Conflict at Colossae: A Problem in the Interpretation of Early Christianity Illustrated by Selected Modern Studies.* SBLSBS 4. Rev. ed. Missoula, Mont.: Scholars Press, 1975. This volume contains an introduction and an epilogue by the editors, plus the following essays: J. B. Lightfoot, "The Colossian Heresy," 13–59; Martin Dibelius, "The Isis Initiation in Apuleius and Related Initiatory Rites," 61–121; Günther Bornkamm, "The Heresy of Colossians," 123–45; Stanislas Lyonnet, S. J., "Paul's Adversaries in Colossae," 147–61; Fred O. Francis, "Humility and Angelic Worship in Col. 2:18," 163–95; and Fred O. Francis, "The Background of EMBATEUEIN (Col 2:18) in Legal Papyri and Oracle Inscriptions," 197–207.

Lohse, Eduard. *Colossians and Philemon.* Trans. William R. Poehlmann and Robert J. Karris. Hermeneia. Philadelphia: Fortress, 1971.

Martin, Ralph P. *Ephesians, Colossians, and Philemon.* Interpretation: A Bible Commentary for Teaching and Preaching. Atlanta: John Knox, 1991.

O'Brien, Peter T. *Colossians, Philemon.* WBC 44. Waco, Tex.: Word, 1982.

Pokorný, Petr. *Colossians: A Commentary.* Trans. Siegfried S. Schatzmann. Peabody, Mass.: Hendrickson, 1991.

Sappington, Thomas J. *Revelation and Redemption at Colossae.* JSNTSup 53. Sheffield: JSOT Press, 1991.

Schweizer, Eduard. *The Letter to the Colossians: A Commentary.* Trans. Andrew Chester. Minneapolis: Augsburg, 1982.

2 Thessalonians

Aus, Roger. *2 Thessalonians.* Augsburg Commentary on the New Testament. Minneapolis: Augsburg, 1984.

Bailey, John. "Who Wrote 2 Thessalonians?" *NTS* 25 (1978): 131–45.

Bassler, Jouette M. "The Enigmatic Sign: 2 Thessalonians 1:5." *CBQ* 46 (1984): 496–510.

Best, Ernest. *A Commentary on the First and Second Epistles to the Thessalonians.* HNTC. New York: Harper & Row, 1972.

Collins, Raymond F., ed. *The Thessalonian Correspondence.* Louvain: University Press, 1990.

Dobschütz, Ernst von. *Die Thessalonicher-Briefe.* Göttingen: Vandenhoeck & Ruprecht, 1909.

Frame, James Everett. *A Critical and Exegetical Commentary on the Epistles of St. Paul to the Thessalonians.* ICC. New York: Scribner's, 1912.

Giblin, Charles H., S.J. *The Threat to Faith. An Exegetical and Theological Reexamination of 2 Thessalonians 2.* AnBib 31. Rome: Pontifical Biblical Institute, 1967.

Holland, Glenn S. *The Tradition that You Received from Us: 2 Thessalonians in the Pauline Tradition* HUT 24. Tübingen: Mohr-Siebeck, 1988.

Hughes, Frank Witt. *Early Christian Rhetoric and 2 Thessalonians.* JSNTSup 30. Sheffield: JSOT Press, 1989.

Jewett, Robert. *The Thessalonian Correspondence: Pauline Rhetoric and Millenarian Piety.* Philadelphia: Fortress, 1986.

Kennedy, George A. *New Testament Interpretation through Rhetorical Criticism.* Chapel Hill: University of North Carolina Press, 1984.

Koester, Helmut. "From Paul's Eschatology to the Apocalyptic Schemata of 2 Thessalonians." In *Thessalonian Correspondence. See* Collins.

Krentz, Edgar. "Traditions Held Fast: Theology and Fidelity in 2 Thessalonians." In *Thessalonian Correspondence. See* Collins.

Krodel, Gerhard. "The Religious Power of Lawlessness; *Katechon* as Precursor of the Lawless One (*Anomos*)," *CurTM* 17 (1990): 440–46.

Laub, Franz. "Paulinische Autorität in nachpaulinischer Zeit (2 Thess)." In *Thessalonian Correspondence. See* Collins.

Lindemann, Andreas. "Zum Abfassungszweck des Zweiten Thessalonicherbriefes." *ZNW* 68 (1977): 35–47.

Malherbe, Abraham J. *Moral Exhortations: A Greco-Roman Sourcebook.* Library of Early Christianity. Philadelphia: Westminster, 1986.

Meeks, Wayne A. *The Moral World of the First Christians.* Library of Early Christianity. Philadelphia: Westminster, 1986.

Milligan, George. *St. Paul's Epistles to the Thessalonians.* London: Macmillan, 1908.

Morris, Leon. *The First and Second Epistles to the Thessalonians.* NICNT. Rev. ed. Grand Rapids: Eerdmans, 1991.

Russell, Ronald. "The Idle in 2 Thess 3:6-12: An Eschatological or a Social Problem?" *NTS* 34 (1988): 105–19.

Schmidt, Daryl. "The Authenticity of 2 Thessalonians: Linguistic Arguments," *SBLSP*, 1983 (Chico, Calif.: SBL, 1983). Pp. 289–96.

———. "1 Thess. 2:13-16: Linguistic Evidence for an Interpolation." *JBL* 102 (1983): 269–79.

———. "The Syntactical Style of 2 Thessalonians: How Pauline Is It?" In *Thessalonian Correspondence. See* Collins.

Strobel, August. *Untersuchungen zum Eschatologischen Verzögerungsproblem auf Grund der spätjüdisch-urchristlichen Geschichte von Habakuk 2:2ff.* NovTSup 2. Leiden: Brill, 1961.

Trilling, Wolfgang. *Untersuchungen zum zweiten Thessalonicherbrief.* ETS 27. Leipzig: St. Benno-Verlag, 1972.

———. *Der zweite Brief an die Thessalonicher.* EKKNT 14. Neukirchen-Vluyn: Neukirchener, 1980.

Wanamaker, Charles A. *The Epistles to the Thessalonians. A Commentary on the Greek Text.* NIGTC. Grand Rapids: Eerdmans, 1990.

1–2 Timothy, Titus

Commentaries and Introductions

Brox, Norbert. *Die Pastoralbriefe.* RNT 7/2. 4th rev. ed. Regensburg: F. Pustet, 1968.

Dibelius, Martin, and Hans Conzelmann. *The Pastoral Epistles.* Trans. Philip Buttolph and Adela Yarbro. Hermeneia. Philadelphia: Fortress, 1972.

Easton, Burton S. *The Pastoral Epistles: Introduction, Translation, Commentary and Word Studies.* New York: Scribner's, 1947.

Fuller, Reginald H. "The Pastoral Epistles." In *Ephesians, Colossians, 2 Thessalonians, The Pastoral Epistles,* ed. Gerhard Krodel. Proclamation Commentaries. Philadelphia: Fortress, 1978. Pp. 97–121.

Guthrie, Donald. *The Pastoral Epistles.* Tyndale New Testament Commentaries. Rev. ed. Grand Rapids: Eerdmans, 1990.

Hanson, Anthony T. *The Pastoral Epistles.* NCBC. Grand Rapids: Eerdmans, 1982.

Holtz, Gottfried. *Die Pastoralbriefe.* THKNT 13. 4th ed. Berlin: Evangelische Verlagsanstalt, 1986.

Hultgren, Arland J. *1 & 2 Timothy, Titus.* Augsburg Commentary on the New Testament. Minneapolis: Augsburg, 1984.

Jeremias, Joachim. *Die Briefe an Timotheus und Titus.* NTD 9. Göttingen: Vandenhoeck & Ruprecht, 1981.

Johnson, Luke T. *The Writings of the New Testament: An Interpretation.* Philadelphia: Fortress, 1986. Pp. 381–407.

Karris, Robert J. *The Pastoral Epistles*. New Testament Message 17. Wilmington, Del.: Michael Glazier, 1979.

Kelly, John N. D. *A Commentary on the Pastoral Epistles*. HNTC. New York: Harper & Row, 1963.

Kümmel, Werner G. *Introduction to the New Testament*. Trans. Howard Clark Kee. Rev. English ed. Nashville: Abingdon, 1975. Pp. 366–87.

Merkel, Helmut. *Die Pastoralbriefe*. NTD 9/1. Göttingen: Vandenhoeck & Ruprecht, 1990.

Quinn, Jerome D. *The Letter to Titus*. AB 35. Garden City, N.Y.: Doubleday, 1990.

Reumann, John. *Variety and Unity in New Testament Thought*. Oxford Bible Series. Oxford: Oxford Univ. Press, 1991. Pp. 129–48.

Roloff, Jürgen. *Der erste Brief an Timotheus*. EKKNT 15. Zurich: Benziger; Neukirchen-Vluyn: Neukirchener, 1988.

Spicq, Ceslaus. *Saint Paul: Les Épîtres Pastorales*. Paris: J. Gabalda, 1969.

Specialized Studies

Fiore, Benjamin. *The Function of Personal Example in the Socratic and Pastoral Epistles*. AnBib 105. Rome: Biblical Institute Press, 1986.

Grayston, K., and G. Herdan. "The Authorship of the Pastorals in the Light of Statistical Linguistics." NTS 6 (1959): 1–15.

Gritz, Sharon Hodgin. *Paul, Women Teachers, and the Mother Goddess at Ephesus: A Study of 1 Timothy 2:9-15 in Light of the Religious and Cultural Milieu of the First Century*. Lanham, Md.: University Press of America, 1991.

Harrison, P. N. *The Problem of the Pastoral Epistles*. London: Oxford, Univ. Press, 1921.

———. *Paulines and Pastorals:* London: Villiers, 1964.

Karris, Robert J. "The Background and Significance of the Polemic of the Pastoral Epistles." *JBL* 92 (1973): 549–64.

Kidd, Reggie M. *Wealth and Beneficence in the Pastoral Epistles*. SBLDS 122. Atlanta: Scholars Press, 1990.

MacDonald, Dennis Ronald. *The Legend and the Apostle: The Battle for Paul in Story and Canon*. Philadelphia: Westminster, 1983.

MacDonald, Margaret Y. *The Pauline Churches: A Socio-historical Study of Institutionalization in the Pauline and Deutero-Pauline Writings*. SNTSMS 60. Cambridge: Cambridge Univ. Press, 1988.

Roller, Otto. *Das Formular der Paulinischen Briefe*. Stuttgart: Kohlhammer, 1933.

Thurston, Bonnie Bowman. *The Widows: A Women's Ministry in the Early Church*. Minneapolis: Fortress, 1989.

Towner, Philip H. *The Goal of Our Instruction: The Structure of Theology and Ethics in the Pastoral Epistles*. JSNTSup 34. Sheffield: JSOT Press, 1989.

Verner, David C. *The Household of God: The Social World of the Pastoral Epistles*. SBLDS 71. Chico, Calif.: Scholars Press, 1983.

Wilson, S. G. *Luke and the Pastoral Epistles*. London: SPCK, 1979.

INDEX